—P E O P L E   T O   K N O W—

FRANKLIN D. ROOSEVELT

The Four-Term President

Michael A. Schuman

ENSLOW PUBLISHERS, INC.

44 Fadem Road	P.O. Box 38
Box 699	Aldershot
Springfield, N.J. 07081	Hants GU12 6BP
U.S.A.	U.K.

> *To Dan Schlossberg, a good friend who helped me get my typewriter in the door way back when.*

Library of Congress Cataloging-in-Publication Data

Schuman, Michael.
    Franklin D. Roosevelt: the four-term president / Michael A. Schuman.
       p. cm. — (People to know)
    Includes bibliographical references (p.) and index.
    Summary: Presents the personal and public life of the thirty-second president of the United States giving particular emphasis to his New Deal programs.
    ISBN 0-89490-696-8
    1. Roosevelt, Franklin D. (Franklin Delano), 1882–1945—Juvenile literature.
2. Presidents—United States —Biography—Juvenile literature. 3. New Deal, 1933–1939—Juvenile literature. 4. United States—History—1933–1945—Juvenile literature. [1. Roosevelt, Franklin D. (Franklin Delano), 1882–1945.
2. Presidents. 3. New Deal, 1933–1939. 4. United States—History—1933–1945.] I. Title. II. Series.
E807.S34 1996
973.917'092—dc20
[B]   95-35211
                                      CIP
                                      AC

Printed in the United States of America

10 9 8 7 6 5 4 3 2 1

Illustration Credits:
Franklin Delano Roosevelt Library, pp. 4, 11, 24, 27, 30, 35, 41, 56, 66, 76, 79, 90, 99, 102; Little White House National Historic Site, p. 50; Michael A. Schuman, p. 43; National Park Service, Roosevelt-Vanderbilt National Historic Sites, Hyde Park, New York, pp. 14, 32, 107.

Cover Illustration:
Franklin Delano Roosevelt Library

Contents

Franklin Delano Roosevelt

1

Election Night

The dawn of November 8, 1932, signaled the start of a new day. But in much of the United States people did not want to get out of bed to face it.

The country was in the midst of its worst crisis since the Civil War. America was deep in a horrible economic depression. It was so severe that many citizens felt that their way of life was doomed. They believed that the country would be unable to weather the economic storm.

In 1932 an astounding 24.1 percent, or nearly a quarter of the country's workers, were unemployed.[1] Without jobs many people had no money. And without money they could not buy food or pay rent. Homeless people were on the streets of every city and town. Average working Americans feared that they might be next to lose their jobs and their homes.

November 8, 1932, was an election day. New York Governor Franklin Delano Roosevelt, a Democrat, was running for President against sitting President Herbert Hoover. At his home in Hyde Park, New York, Roosevelt woke up and went to the Hyde Park town hall. There he and his wife, Eleanor, cast their votes. Later that day the Roosevelts traveled ninety-five miles south to New York City, where they maintained another home.

Just eleven years earlier Franklin Roosevelt would have seemed an unlikely presidential candidate. In August 1921, he contracted polio, a disease that attacks the nervous system. In November 1921, he was bedridden with paralyzed legs. His main concern was trying to live a normal life. Running for President seemed an impossible dream.

Through determination and courage, Roosevelt strengthened his upper body and learned to get around as best as he could. He carved out a political career as a state leader. During the campaign of 1932, he cultivated an image of a man brimming with confidence.

As the afternoon of November 8 turned into evening, the Roosevelts ate a buffet supper with some close friends in their New York City home. After dinner they went to the Biltmore Hotel in New York and waited for the election returns to be tallied.

Polls indicated that Roosevelt would win. But one of his most trusted advisors, Louis Howe, was pessimistic.

When Roosevelt took an early lead, Howe said, "Losers always have a big spurt before they dwindle off to defeat."[2]

This time the lead did not dwindle. As more election returns came in, it was clear that the American people were putting their faith in a new leader. Roosevelt won the election by a landslide, capturing forty-two of the forty-eight states. (Alaska and Hawaii were not yet states.) Shortly after midnight President Hoover conceded defeat. Roosevelt went to the hotel ballroom and gave a victory speech. He then released the following statement:

> While I am grateful with all my heart for this expression of the confidence of my fellow Americans, I realize keenly the responsibility I shall assume and I mean to serve with my utmost capacity the interest of the nation.[3]

The public was anxious for Franklin Delano Roosevelt, who would become known by his initials FDR, to take over the job of President. With his winning smile, powerful words, and confident manner, Franklin Roosevelt had earned the trust of the American people. Roosevelt had been chosen to bring the United States out of despair.

No one could have imagined the conversation the President-elect had with his grown son James in his private bedroom in the Roosevelt family home that election night.

James remembered:

As I kissed him good night he looked up at me. . .
'You know, Jimmy,' he said, 'all my life I have
been afraid of only one thing—fire. Tonight I
think I'm afraid of something else.'

'Afraid of what, Pa?' I said.

'I'm just afraid,' he said, 'that I may not have
the strength to do this job.'

'After you leave me tonight, Jimmy,' he went
on, 'I am going to pray. I am going to pray that
God will help me, that He will give me the
strength and the guidance to do this job and to do
it right. I hope you will pray for me, too, Jimmy.'

I stood there for a moment, unable to say
anything. Then I left Father alone in his room,
about to embark on the great loneliness of the
Presidency. I went to my room and did as he had
asked me.[4]

A Strange Wish
for a Young Man

America's Presidents have come from a variety of backgrounds. Some—such as Abraham Lincoln, Harry Truman, and Dwight Eisenhower—were born and raised in humble surroundings. They had to work hard as young people to help their families pay bills. And they often lived in small crowded houses.

Others—such as Theodore Roosevelt, John F. Kennedy, and George Bush—grew up in very comfortable settings. They lived in handsome houses or even mansions. They may have had paid servants to help with family chores. Their parents were able to afford to send them to the best private schools and colleges.

Franklin Delano Roosevelt grew up in the latter category. His ancestors on both his father's and mother's sides had been in America since the 1600s. Franklin spend his earliest years in a plush mansion called Springwood in the town of Hyde Park, New York.

Young Franklin was a very pampered boy, although at first it seemed as though he would never have a chance to live. He was born on January 30, 1882. At birth he did not move and was bluish in color. He appeared not to be alive. Immediately the attending doctor, Edward H. Parker, placed his mouth on Franklin's and blew air into the baby's lungs. At first the infant took a few uneasy breaths, then he finally let out a full cry.

Franklin's father, James, made a note of the birth in his wife Sara's diary. He made no mention of the trouble. He simply wrote, "At quarter to nine my Sallie had a splendid large baby boy. He weighs 10 lbs [pounds] without clothes."[1]

But he did discuss the problem birth with a relative, Ellen Roosevelt, in a quick note he wrote that evening. "I have only a moment to write you that Sallie has a bouncing boy; poor child, she has had a very hard time."[2] (James was twice the age of his wife, which is possibly why he referred to her as "poor child.")

Because of his wealthy background, Franklin had a childhood different from that of most young people. He thought nothing of cruising to Europe with his parents whenever they wished. In warm months he sailed with his parents to their summer home on an island called Campobello. The island was just across the Maine border in the Canadian province of New Brunswick.

Franklin Delano Roosevelt, age one, sits on his father's shoulder.

Because both his mother's and father's families had long-standing and distinguished backgrounds in the United States, Franklin was brought up in the proper manners of high society. For a small boy, that meant he had little free will. Every moment of his day was scheduled and supervised. The idea of leaving young children to amuse themselves or to play with friends without adult supervision was unheard of during that time.

Franklin was awakened every morning at 7:00 A.M. He had breakfast at 8:00, then morning lessons with a private governess. Next he had lunch and more lessons until 4:00 P.M. From 4:00 until 6:00 P.M. he was permitted to play supervised games, first approved by his mother. Dinner was at 6:00; and bedtime at 8:00 P.M. That was his schedule every day—day after day after day.

When Franklin was four a distant cousin of his father, named Elliot Roosevelt, came to visit at Springwood. Elliot brought with him his wife and two-year-old daughter Anna Eleanor, who was called Eleanor. Franklin enjoyed being with his new young friend. He spent much of the time playfully carrying Eleanor on his back in the nursery, back and forth across the room.

Franklin tried never to disagree with his parents and usually kept his feelings to himself. This may have stemmed from the manners of his class taught to him by his parents. It was not proper—especially for a boy—to complain, cry, or show any kind of raw emotion.

One day though, when Franklin was about eight, he displayed anger at his parents because of his strict schedule. He told his mother that he wanted his freedom. She replied that he could do whatever he wished for one day, except for meals, which would still be scheduled.

Sara said he came back that day "a very dirty, tired youngster." But he did not complain, discuss his feelings, or tell her what he did on that one day of freedom.[3]

Naturally, James and Sara Roosevelt's friends were in the same social class as they were. As a boy, when Franklin traveled with his parents, he met the types of people other children could only dream of. This included world leaders, royalty, and famous authors such as Mark Twain. Franklin even was able to visit the White House in 1887 when he was five years old. There he met President Grover Cleveland.

Like Franklin's parents, President Cleveland was also from New York State and a Democrat. Cleveland had offered James Roosevelt any of several diplomatic posts. Not wanting any part of public life, Franklin's father rejected them all.

When Franklin and his father were leaving the White House that day, President Cleveland said something to the five-year-old boy that has become legendary. He told him, "My little man, I am making a

13

As a boy, Franklin Roosevelt learned how to ride a horse and sail from his father. Here, Franklin is shown with his parents, James and Sara Roosevelt.

strange wish for you. It is that you may never be President of the United States."[4]

Franklin remembered President Cleveland as being weary and discouraged that day.[5] But in spite of what Cleveland said, he could not have hated his job very much. He ran for President two more times. He lost reelection in 1888, but ran again in 1892 and won. Cleveland became the only United States President to serve nonconsecutive terms.

Franklin's childhood was unusual in another way. Franklin had no brothers or sisters, so he received undivided attention from his wealthy parents. (He did have a half-brother named James, who was twenty-eight years older than Franklin. James was born to Franklin's father and his first wife, Rebecca, who died. Franklin's father later married Sara Delano, his mother.)

Franklin had a few friends his age who were also the children of wealthy parents. His best friend, a boy named Archie Rogers, Jr., died at age seven of a disease called diphtheria. The disease causes membranes to grow in the throat, making breathing difficult. It was a frequent illness of Franklin's day, but today is easily controlled by a vaccine. Typically, Franklin did not discuss his grief with anyone.

In spite of his few friends, much of Franklin's boyhood was spent with adults. He was shy, but became very comfortable with adults and learned how to charm them. This was a trait that would help later when he was in politics. On one occasion one of his aunts praised him for his tact. In response, Franklin said, "Yes, I'm just chuck full of tacks!"[6] That drew a smile from his aunt.

Franklin also began showing signs of another skill needed for a life as the take-charge political leader he would become. Sometimes Franklin's parents allowed him to play with the children of the people who worked for them. Franklin loved horses and especially liked being with the family's stable boys. However, he always made certain that he was the one in charge of their play activities. He gave all the orders.

One day his mother told Franklin that it would be nice to let some of his friends give orders too.

Franklin responded, "Mummie, if I didn't give the orders, nothing would happen!"[7]

When most boys of Franklin's social class got older, they continued their education away from home at a private boarding school. Many went as early as age twelve, but Franklin was not sent until he was fourteen. Sara delayed separating herself from her only child as long as she could. Even when he finally left for school, she wrote in her diary, "It is hard to leave my darling boy."[8]

Franklin attended classes and lived at the exclusive Groton School in Groton, Massachusetts. All the students were boys and the vast majority, like Franklin, were from wealthy families. The furnishings and surroundings were comfortable, but much plainer than the mansions and estates where the students had grown. One boy, a son of a millionaire, was found crying on his first day of school. When asked what was the matter he sobbed that the stairs had no carpets covering them.

Many young people who leave home for the first time—whether to go to camp, boarding school, or college—have trouble adjusting. Franklin was no different. He was a good student, but not exceptional. However, he wanted to be popular among the other students; and a major key to popularity at Groton was being skilled at sports. Even the rector (equal to a principal), an aristocratic man named Reverend Endicott Peabody, had immense respect for students who were good athletes. He especially admired football players.

Peabody said that he "trusted a football player more than a non-football player, just as the boys did." He added that football "is of profound importance for the morale, even more than for the physical development of the boys. In these days of exceeding comfort, the boys need an opportunity to endure hardness and, it may be, suffering."[9]

Because he was very thin for his age, Franklin was not a good athlete—at least not at sports that counted, such as football and baseball. When he entered Groton he was only five feet three inches and weighed barely one hundred pounds. He eventually would grow to be six feet one inch.

Franklin did have some talent at tennis and golf, but

individual sports were not as important as team sports at Groton. Franklin, always the center of attention at home, was uneasy about not being popular and a school leader.

In his final year, Franklin became manager of the baseball team. The position was more of an equipment manager than a field manager. But he did win an athletic ribbon for his services to the team. Still it was an empty honor since most praise went to the athletes and not the manager.

There were other reasons why Franklin had trouble adjusting to the halls of Groton. One was because of a fellow student—his half-nephew James Roosevelt Roosevelt, Jr., nicknamed "Taddy." Taddy was the son of Franklin's half-brother James. Although Taddy was Franklin's half-nephew, he was three years older than Franklin.

Taddy was poor at both sports and studies. He had trouble with simple tasks. To his classmates he seemed to be a social misfit, unable to carry on an intelligent conversation. Taddy was extremely unpopular and was constantly teased. Once the boys discovered that Franklin was related to Taddy, they teased him as well. Franklin tried to ignore the insults, but they made his adjustment at school more difficult.

In addition, Franklin entered Groton at age fourteen. Considering that most other boys entered at age twelve they had already formed friendships. It was hard for Franklin to break into these established cliques and make friends of his own.

Over the course of his four years at Groton, Franklin became more accepted, though he never really shined as a school leader. To achieve success at sports, he took boxing lessons and was classified as a lightweight. Franklin fought a bruising two-round battle against a boy named Fuller Potter in a school tournament. Fuller won the match by a decision, even though both boys wound up with bloody noses and cut lips at the fight's end.

Four decades later, when Roosevelt was President of the United States, Potter was a successful broker on Wall Street and a diehard Republican. Roosevelt grumbled jokingly, "I should have hit him one more time."[10]

In his last year at Groton, Franklin was named a dormitory prefect. His main responsibility was to keep tabs on the younger boys and make sure that they stayed in line. With the job came the honor of a private study. He did this job well and earned the respect of most of the newly arrived students he supervised.

In addition to his efforts at extracurricular activities, Franklin studied hard and continued to earn good grades. He polished skills that would help him as an adult in politics. With practice, he became a talented debater and public speaker.

Franklin was also heavily influenced by a guest speaker who came to Groton. He was an

African-American attorney from a predominantly black college in Virginia called the Hampton Institute. It is likely that Franklin had never seen an African American who was not a servant, and he was very impressed at this man's accomplishments.[11] In fact, after hearing him speak, Franklin donated fifty cents to the Hampton Institute. Then he wrote to his parents for permission to contribute another fifty cents.

Away from school Franklin stayed in touch with the family of his distant cousin Theodore, by then the governor of New York. Theodore Roosevelt's home was a mansion called Sagamore Hill in Oyster Bay, New York, on Long Island. Though the members of the Oyster Bay branch of the family were Republicans, the Roosevelts did not let politics come between them. Franklin greatly admired Theodore and gladly attended the family's parties and get-togethers. At the family Christmas party in 1898, when Franklin was sixteen, he again met Eleanor.

Eleanor, at fourteen, was uncomfortable at parties. She felt that she was homely and was self-conscious about her looks.[12] Her mother, Anna Hall Roosevelt, was a very beautiful woman, and Eleanor believed that her mother looked down on her because she was not pretty. Anna nicknamed Eleanor "Granny" because she tended to act old-fashioned in her ways. Though her mother may not have meant the nickname as an insult, Eleanor took it in that manner.[13] She wrote that she "wanted to sink through the floor in shame."[14]

Eleanor also wrote that her mother said she should learn proper manners to compensate for her lack of physical beauty. This only made Eleanor feel more uncomfortable about the way she looked.[15]

Years later Eleanor remembered this particular Christmas dance. She wrote:

> I was a poor dancer, and the climax of the party was a dance. I still remember the inappropriate dresses I wore—and, worse of all they were above my knees. I knew, of course, I was different from all the other girls and if I had not known, they were frank in telling me so! I still remember my gratitude at one of these parties to my cousin Franklin Roosevelt when he came and asked me to dance with him![16]

It might seem unusual today that a teenager would feel awkward wearing dresses cut above the knees. But in Eleanor's time, short dresses were unfashionable and seemed more appropriate for small children.

Franklin, on the other hand, loved parties. He was a handsome young man with a slender build and hair parted in the middle. He enjoyed flirting with girls, and many girls liked him. One girl whom he enjoyed being with was Eleanor. "Cousin Eleanor has a very good mind," he told his mother.[17] He would be meeting Eleanor again, just a few years later.

Marriage, Politics, and a Car with No Windshield

As 1899 turned into 1900 and the nineteenth century became the twentieth, there were major changes in the life of Franklin Roosevelt and his family. In November 1900, distant cousin Theodore was elected Vice President of the United States. He was the running mate of William McKinley, who was reelected to a second term as President. Though Franklin's branch of the family was loyal to the Democrats, Franklin actively supported his Republican cousin.

Two months prior to the election, Roosevelt entered Harvard University in Cambridge, Massachusetts. At Groton he had taken courses as part of an "anticipation plan," which was similar to an early admissions plan. With this program, Roosevelt took courses for which he would be given credit at Harvard. Because he had completed these courses, he would be able to graduate Harvard in three years instead of the usual four.

Unlike his years at Groton, at Harvard, Roosevelt achieved his desire to be popular. Skill in sports was not the main gateway to social success among these older and more mature students. However, Roosevelt still tried out for the Harvard football team. Although he was too thin for the varsity team, he did make a freshman scrub team.

Roosevelt achieved his popularity by taking part in a number of political, social, and extracurricular activities. He made his biggest impression as president (equal to an editor-in-chief) of Harvard's newspaper the *Crimson*. With a cousin named Roosevelt recently elected as Vice President of the United States, Franklin's last name also became a boost to his image. Some even thought he was the Vice President's nephew.

There was one potential block to the approval of his fellow students. His half-nephew Taddy was now a student at Harvard and was just as much of an embarrassment as he had been at Groton.[1] The biggest humiliation came in the fall of Franklin's freshman year. It was leaked to the press that Taddy had married a New York City prostitute a few months earlier.[2] The fact that Franklin was related to the Vice President may have offset the association with his shameful half-nephew, since Franklin did not suffer the same social setbacks as he did at Groton.

There may have been some repercussions, however.

Franklin Roosevelt lived in this dormitory room while attending Harvard University.

Roosevelt had his heart set on being admitted to an exclusive Harvard social club called Porcellian. But he was not accepted. One of Franklin's cousins later said that Franklin told him the rejection was "the greatest disappointment he ever had."[3]

Some historians have speculated that he was tainted by his relationship with his half-nephew Taddy. In spite of this setback, Roosevelt enjoyed his years at college.[4] He could have graduated after three years, but stayed for a fourth so he could work as the *Crimson*'s editor.

There was one tragic occurrence during Roosevelt's college years. His father died at age seventy-two on December 7, 1900. Ironically, the date December 7 would take on a major significance in his life again—forty-one years later.

To help his mother through her loneliness, Franklin spent the next summer traveling with her, a cousin, and another family throughout Europe. While in Paris they received word that back in the United States President McKinley had been shot in Buffalo, New York, on September 6, 1901.

McKinley was operated on and at first seemed as though he would recover. But while the Roosevelts were sailing home on September 18, the crew of a passing lightship announced through a megaphone that McKinley had died. Franklin's cousin Theodore Roosevelt was now President of the United States.

Franklin said that he always remembered the words

cousin Theodore said to him. "The only real danger from an assassin is from one who does not care whether he loses his own life in the act or not. Most of the crazy ones can be spotted first."[5]

The assassin in this case was a first-generation American laborer and anarchist named Leon Czolgosz. Anarchism is a theory that all forms of government are oppressive and should be abolished. Czolgosz said that he had no personal dislike for McKinley, but as an anarchist, he was against all government leaders. Czolgosz was found guilty of murdering the President and was electrocuted less than two months after the attack.

Back at Harvard, Roosevelt continued with his studies, extracurricular activities, and social life. He dated many young women, some seriously. One was Dorothy Quincy, a beautiful woman who often accompanied him to football games and dinners. On December 12, 1902, they went together to dinner and a dance. Roosevelt wrote in his diary, "everything was glorious. Got back at 6 A.M. Didn't go to bed."[6]

Another was Alice Sohier, who was also very attractive. Her father was a former Massachusetts Republican state legislator. Franklin cared deeply about Alice and she enjoyed being with him.[7]

But Franklin and Alice did not marry. It is not known why, although some speculate that she did not want to have a large family as Franklin desired. As a

Franklin Roosevelt, at the age of twenty-one, was popular in school
and dated several women.

child, Alice had been weak and seemed to catch every childhood illness that came her way. Perhaps she did not think she was in the proper physical condition to have the many children Franklin wanted.[8]

Not all women admired Franklin. Some thought he talked too much and tried too hard to be perfect. Others, including Eleanor's first cousin Alice, felt that he was under control of his mother and was a "mother's boy."[9] Some said that the first two initials of his name stood for "feather duster," a term meaning someone of limited ability and intelligence.

One of the many who did admire Franklin was cousin Eleanor. They saw each other at dances and parties during the summer of 1902. And they continued their relationship during the following school year when Franklin came home on visits from Harvard. In the summer of 1903 Eleanor visited Franklin at Campobello. She was accompanied by a chaperone. In that day it was considered improper for an unmarried woman to visit a man on her own.

Despite Eleanor's belief that she was homely, several men besides Franklin found her attractive. But beneath the skin, she and Franklin had much in common. They had the same backgrounds and the same values—mainly a concern for the poor and other oppressed minorities.

Meanwhile, Roosevelt formally graduated Harvard with the class of 1904. He had applied and was accepted at Columbia University Law School in New York City. He began attending classes there in 1904.

Franklin and Eleanor Roosevelt were married on March 17, 1905 (Saint Patrick's Day), while Franklin was in his first year in law school. Eleanor's Uncle Ted, who had won reelection as President of the United States in 1904, gave away the bride. Reverend Endicott Peabody, the rector from Groton, performed the ceremony.

"Well, Franklin," said the President at the wedding, "there's nothing like keeping the name in the family."[10]

Following a honeymoon in Europe, the young couple settled in New York City, with Franklin's mother living just three blocks away. Franklin finished his second year of law school. He then passed the New York State Bar examination and decided there was no need to complete law school. Instead, he went to work as a lawyer with a prestigious firm on Wall Street in New York City's financial district.

Eleanor immediately began filling the traditional roles of wife and mother. In 1906 she and Franklin had their first baby, a girl named Anna Eleanor for her mother. The next year Eleanor gave birth to a boy named James, in memory of Franklin's father. In 1909 she had another baby, a boy named Franklin, Jr. Tragically the boy contracted influenza, a viral disease, and died when he was just seven months old. A third son, Elliott, was born in 1910.

Newlyweds Franklin and Eleanor Roosevelt honeymooned in Europe after their 1905 wedding.

Roosevelt was not enthusiastic about his work as a lawyer. The example set by cousin Theodore, who was a strong and popular President, helped convince Franklin to enter politics. Theodore himself had asked that "young fellows of our sort" enter politics.[11]

When a regional politician asked Franklin to run for state senator from Hyde Park in the spring of 1910, the young attorney happily said yes. Nobody would have reasonably predicted that Roosevelt would win. First, he was only twenty-eight years old, which was very young to hold political office. Second, Hyde Park and most of New York State outside New York City was heavily Republican. Although he had voted for his Republican cousin for Vice President, and later President, Franklin still considered himself a Democrat. Yet no Democrat had been elected state senator from his district in fifty-four years.

The area around Hyde Park was mostly rural in 1910, and Roosevelt ran as a friend of farmers. The fact that his Hyde Park home was a comfortable mansion seemed to make little difference. Roosevelt also stressed honesty and frequently invoked the name of his widely loved cousin Theodore, by then an ex-President.

Roosevelt and two other Democratic candidates for local office rented a car and drove throughout the district, campaigning at places farmers gathered. At this time cars were still relatively new and very basic. Roosevelt's car had no top and no windshield. Since

Franklin Roosevelt's Hyde Park home was a comfortable mansion, yet he ran as a friend of farmers in the 1910 election.

most roads in the district were dirt, he and his staff had to wear raincoats or smocks to keep their clothes clean.

Roosevelt learned campaigning techniques from the older and more experienced candidates. He took the advice of one fellow candidate, Richard Connell, who suggested that he refer to his gathered audience as "my friends." By doing this he was including himself as one of them.

Out of approximately thirty thousand votes cast, Roosevelt won the election by just over one thousand votes. He moved his family to Albany, the state capital, and a long and illustrious political career was begun.

It was in Albany that Roosevelt met a newspaper correspondent named Louis Howe. Howe was a politically savvy man who saw a lot of promise in the young Roosevelt. Howe offered his services to Roosevelt, who hired him as an advisor.

Roosevelt did not stay long in Albany. Woodrow Wilson, a Democrat, was elected President in 1912 in an unusual three-man race. One of the candidates was sitting President William Howard Taft. The third was former President Theodore Roosevelt, running on a third party called the Progressive, or Bull Moose, party.

Theodore Roosevelt had become disenchanted with Taft, a fellow Republican. He felt that Taft had abandoned the progressive policies he had championed. So the ex-President created his own third party to reflect his personal views. With the Republican vote now split between Theodore Roosevelt and Taft, Wilson easily won.

Franklin campaigned hard for Wilson and was rewarded with an important position in Wilson's administration, the assistant secretary of the Navy. It was a major step for a relatively inexperienced politician. It was also a position that cousin Theodore held before he became President. Franklin moved to Washington, D.C., with his family. He also asked Louis Howe, by now a friend as well as advisor, to come with him and be his assistant for the new job.

Roosevelt had always been an admirer of all things nautical and he showed it in his new position. He proved highly capable in carrying out his duties, such as solving problems in naval contracts and inspecting ships. After learning that many sailors could not swim and some had drowned at sea, Roosevelt made it mandatory that all Navy personnel pass a swimming test before taking to the ocean.

While in Washington, Eleanor gave birth to two more children. She had a fourth son in 1914. He was named Franklin, Jr., in memory of the boy who died in 1909.

That same year war broke out in Europe. It would last four years and became known as World War I. The basic causes were rivalries among the countries of Europe and long-standing ethnic hatred among people of different backgrounds.

Louis Howe became Franklin Roosevelt's advisor and friend.

One major event that lead to the war was the assassination of Archduke Franz Ferdinand, the heir to the throne of Austria-Hungary, on June 28, 1914. (Today Austria and Hungary are two separate countries.) The assassin was a teenager named Gavrilo Princip who was a nationalist from Serbia, a country south of Austria-Hungary.

Within a month Austria-Hungary invaded Serbia in retaliation for the assassination. Nearly every other country in Europe took one side or another, and by the end of the year, Europe was engulfed in all-out war. The main countries that supported Serbia were Great Britain, France, and Russia. Those supporting Austria-Hungary included Germany, Turkey, and Bulgaria.

At first the United States remained neutral. President Wilson won reelection in 1916 with the slogan "He kept us out of war." For the Roosevelt family, there was one more reason to celebrate that year. Eleanor and Franklin's last child, a son named John, was born.

By 1917 war activities were causing Americans to feel threatened. One reason was repeated German submarine attacks on Allied vessels, including American merchant ships.

Another was a message called the Zimmermann Note. Earlier that year, the German foreign minister sent a note to the German ambassador to Mexico. The Zimmermann Note, as it was called, was intercepted by the Allies. It instructed the German ambassador to try to persuade Mexico to declare war on the United States. In exchange Germany would give Mexico financial aid and arrange to return Texas, New Mexico, and Arizona to Mexico. Those three states had at one time been part of Mexico.

After the Allies made the Zimmermann Note public, Americans felt that their fears of Germany were justified. The United States officially entered into the war in April 1917.

Roosevelt had a major role in readying the United States Navy for its war effort. Unlike his indifferent attitude toward his work as a lawyer, Roosevelt loved his Navy post.[12] This showed when he performed at his job.

He was instrumental in modernizing the Navy. He ordered the building of hundreds of new ships and the recruitment of thousands of additional service people. Roosevelt worked very capably under extreme pressure during the war. By the time the war ended on November 11, 1918, FDR had made a name for himself.

But there had been a major development in his personal life that was kept from the general public. While the Roosevelts seemed to be a large happy family on the outside, Franklin and Eleanor came very close to divorce in 1918.

Eleanor discovered love letters written between Franklin and her social secretary Lucy Mercer. The two were involved in a romantic affair. Eleanor offered Franklin a divorce, but he declined. Divorce at the time was not as accepted as it is today and could have been devastating to a political career. Franklin promised that he would never see Lucy again, and Franklin and Eleanor stayed married.[13]

Meanwhile the treaty outlining terms for the end of World War I was being hammered out in Versailles, France. One condition of the Treaty of Versailles was the formation of an organization called the League of Nations. It allowed countries of the world to gather and openly discuss their disputes for the purpose of preventing war. Basically it was a forerunner of today's United Nations (UN).

The League of Nations became a major issue in the 1920 presidential election. President Wilson and Roosevelt both strongly supported it.

One politician who did not support the League of Nations was Ohio Governor James M. Cox, the Democratic nominee for President in 1920. In order to balance the ticket, Cox felt that his running mate should be a supporter of the League. He selected Roosevelt.

Following the tumult of World War I, Americans were tired of involvement in other countries' problems. They wanted to live normal lives again and not become entangled in international affairs. Many Americans felt that membership in the League of Nations would force the United States to get involved. The Republican candidates, Warren G. Harding and Calvin Coolidge, both opposed United States membership in the league.

They ran on the slogan "Return to Normalcy." Their strategy paid off. Harding and Coolidge won in a landslide.

Roosevelt wrote at the time:

> I am not really much surprised at the result, because I have felt all along that we are in the middle of a kind of tidal flow of discontent and destructive criticism, as a result of the tremendous efforts of the war.[14]

In spite of the defeat, Roosevelt's name was now known to even more people, and his national star was rising.

Portrait of Courage

Roosevelt, too, tried to return to a life of normalcy following his marital crisis and his election loss. In 1921 he returned to New York City, where he and Eleanor continued raising their five surviving children. Roosevelt took a job outside of public life as vice president of a banking firm. Although the banking job earned Roosevelt money, it seemed secondary to his real passions: keeping his name in the public eye and rebuilding his political career.

The Roosevelts still used their vacation home on Campobello Island as an escape from the city. They planned a visit in August 1921. But first on July 27, FDR, along with several dignitaries, made a visit to a Boy Scout camp in a forest north of New York City.

Then, on August 5, he set sail aboard a boat called

On July 27, 1921, Franklin Roosevelt visited a Boy Scout camp in Bear Mountain, New York.

the *Sabalo* for Campobello. He arrived on August 7. There to meet him were Eleanor, their children, and Louis Howe. Roosevelt and Howe had planned to discuss the upcoming elections of 1922. Nobody could have known that the lives of all involved were about to be changed forever.

According to Leslie Watson, curator of Roosevelt-Campobello International Park, "On August 9 Roosevelt and his employer were using the *Sabalo* and Roosevelt fell off the boat into the frigid North Atlantic waters. He later said, 'The water was so cold it seemed paralyzing.'"[1]

The next day, August 10, he took his children sailing on another boat. While at sea they saw a forest fire on a small island. They docked the boat and helped extinguish the fire. Covered with grime and ashes and smelling of smoke, Roosevelt returned to Campobello and took a swim in an inland lake. Without changing out of his wet bathing suit, he jogged about two miles back to the cottage. He then took another swim in the cold waters of the Bay of Fundy.

Roosevelt entered the cottage living room and read some newspapers that had arrived in the mail. Feeling chilled, he skipped dinner and went straight to bed. The first sign that something was seriously wrong occurred that night when Roosevelt woke to the use the bathroom. He fell out of bed, and Eleanor discovered him crawling on his hands and knees.

Campobello was a place where Franklin Roosevelt and family spent many leisure hours.

The next morning, August 11, Roosevelt woke and found his left leg would hardly move. A check of his temperature showed that he had a fever of 102°F. Eleanor summoned a doctor from the mainland village of Lubec, Maine. The doctor examined Roosevelt and said that he had only a common cold.

Roosevelt's health got worse. On the following morning, August 12, he was completely paralyzed from the waist down. Just three days earlier he had described the cold waters as "paralyzing" after falling from the *Sabalo*.

Another doctor was called. He first diagnosed Roosevelt's illness as a blood clot in the lower spinal cord. Then he changed his mind and said that the problem was a lesion. The doctor prescribed massage, and Eleanor and Louis Howe vigorously massaged Franklin's injured legs for two weeks.

Roosevelt's symptoms worsened. Still another doctor, a specialist from Boston named Dr. Robert W. Lovett, was sent to Campobello. Lovett right away confirmed that Roosevelt had poliomyelitis, also known as infantile paralysis or polio. The constant massage had not only caused Roosevelt agonizing pain, but had severely damaged his already weakened leg muscles.

Polio is a contagious disease that attacks people's nervous systems, often leaving them paralyzed. Usually children, not adults like Roosevelt, were the sufferers. In the 1950s two research scientists, Jonas Salk and Albert

Sabin, each developed separate vaccines to prevent polio. Today in the United States, children are regularly vaccinated to prevent this illness, and cases are very rare. But in the 1920s there was no such way of preventing polio.

It is not known exactly where Roosevelt was infected by the polio virus, but most historians believe that it was at the Boy Scout camp. Leslie Watson of Roosevelt-Campobello International Park says:

> Our staff conducted interviews with the Roosevelt children in the 1970s and learned that some of the children and cottage staff exhibited symptoms of polio at the same time, though only FDR got a full fledged case. One maid said she felt sluggish for several days. Some of the children were bedridden and some threw up. It's possible that Franklin's immunities were down after he overexerted himself by running in wet clothes and swimming in cold water. Whether he would have gotten polio otherwise is the great unknown.[2]

Life for polio patients at the time was doubly troubling. First, there was the physical distress. But polio was a much feared disease, and there was an emotional disgrace to those infected with it. It was typical for residents living in a house with a polio victim to place a sign on a front window, warning strangers to stay away.

Biographer Geoffrey Ward said of Roosevelt:

> For a man as energetic, who had led such a charmed life, to be suddenly paralyzed must have

been almost unbearable. He asked Louis Howe why God had deserted him at one point. He tried to put on a brave front with the children but he was terrified . . . certainly it was the blackest moment of his life and seemed to be the end of his life.[3]

After about a month at Campobello, Roosevelt was moved to a hospital in New York City. At the end of October he was discharged and went home. The following June, in 1922, he moved back to Springwood in Hyde Park. This man, who hoped to lead people, spent his days learning to sit up. He could barely get around on his own, and only with crutches or a wheelchair. While inside he may have been scared, on the outside he wore a brave face.[4]

Eleanor, meanwhile, stayed with Franklin and constantly cared for him. When he first showed signs of the sickness at Campobello, she was by his side twenty-four hours a day, attending to his every need. At their New York City and Hyde Park homes she had a running battle with Sara over who would take better care of Franklin.

A year went by and Roosevelt was no better. One outcome seemed certain—his political career was finished. Now Roosevelt's main concern in life was not running for national office, but learning how to walk.

Roosevelt's doctors told him that the only chance he had of getting better was through rigorous exercise. Those who referred to him as "feather duster" and "mother's boy" would have been surprised. Roosevelt was a portrait of strength, courage, and determination. He had parallel bars installed on the Hyde Park lawn so that he could better develop his upper body. He took hot baths to improve circulation in his legs. And he looked toward the future and set specific goals.

One goal was to be able to walk on crutches the entire length of the Springwood driveway, which was about one-quarter of a mile long. He fell often and much of the time would have to wait on the ground until someone came to help him up. Daughter Anna, by then a teenager, recalled hearing her father urge himself on, saying, "I must get down the driveway today—all the way down the driveway."[5]

Outwardly Roosevelt never felt sorry for himself. At times he talked about his polio with a sense of humor. He might end a conversation with, "Good-bye. I've got to run." On other occasions he would refer to something humorous as "funny as a crutch."[6]

In the fall of 1922, Roosevelt returned to his banking job in New York City. At first he went to the office twice a week. Gradually he increased his work schedule to four days a week. Even though there was only one step leading from the street to his office building, climbing it was still a difficult feat for Roosevelt.

Sara Roosevelt wanted her son to retire to Springwood, where he would not have to work. But

Eleanor and Louis Howe felt differently. They thought that Franklin would be happier if he stayed active.[7]

In the fall of 1924 Roosevelt learned about a run-down resort in the village of Warm Springs in western Georgia. The steaming mineral water that came up from the ground there was said to have wonderful healing powers. Roosevelt started visiting Warm Springs, where he would regularly swim.

Roosevelt enjoyed both the waters and the relaxing atmosphere so much that he invested $200,000 of his money into rehabilitating the resort. The sum was about two-thirds of his private fortune.[8]

The rehabilitated resort was to be called the Georgia Warm Springs Foundation. It became the first modern treatment center for polio, and sufferers of the disease from throughout the United States went there. As the foundation became better known, more people donated money to construct new or to improve existing facilities.

The Georgia resort replaced Campobello as Roosevelt's second home. Because of the bad memories, Campobello became associated with tragedy, and Roosevelt rarely went back there. At his new vacation home he laughed and smiled with patients. At times one or two members of his family might join him.

Roosevelt's son James wrote that many there felt sorry for FDR at first, but his optimism put an end to feelings of pity:

In the pool . . . Father became not just a 'polio'

(victim), but 'Doctor' Roosevelt, a persuasive, confidence-inspiring figure, who was delighted to teach other victims how to do the restorative exercises he had painstakingly learned, including some he had developed on his own.[9]

Whether Roosevelt would be able to salvage any kind of public career was in doubt. But he would not give up trying. Howe urged Eleanor to get involved in politics. There were two reasons for this. First, it would keep Franklin interested in political goings-on. Second, it would keep the Roosevelt name in the public eye.

Eleanor worked closely with the Women's Division of the Democratic State Committee of New York. She became active in groups involved with women's rights, such as the League of Women Voters and Women's Trade Union League.

Franklin's first major public appearance after contracting polio was at the 1924 Democratic Convention at Madison Square Garden in New York City. Like all conventions, it was held during the summer. But this was long before air-conditioning became commonplace. The weather was brutally humid, and the participants inside were baking in torrid heat.

Roosevelt was scheduled to make a nominating speech for New York Governor Al Smith. Any fall or slip by Roosevelt while making his way from the convention floor to or from the podium would have been humiliating. It could even have been fatal to any continued life

The Georgia resort in Warm Springs became Roosevelt's second
home. Shown here is the living room and the chair where Roosevelt
used to sit.

in politics. Roosevelt could not be seen in a wheelchair and still be taken seriously as a future candidate for national office. A person in a wheelchair would not project an image of strength.

Roosevelt had an added challenge of trying to hold an audience's attention while standing on steel braces. Would the braces be so uncomfortable that Roosevelt would be unable to concentrate on his speech and make his words compelling?

Roosevelt's son James, then sixteen, helped him to his seat before each day of the convention and off the floor whenever he wished to leave. When it was nearing Roosevelt's time to speak, James helped his father to the rear of the platform.

Though his son helped him to the stage, Roosevelt made up his mind that he would walk by himself to the rostrum.[10] Before rising he asked a colleague to shake the rostrum to be certain it would support his weight, since he would have to lean on it heavily.

James remembered, ". . . as he reached the rostrum, came this tremendous, roaring ovation. At that moment, I was so damned proud of him that it was with difficulty that I kept myself from bursting into tears."[11]

The audience cheered wildly. Roosevelt tore into his speech. He praised Smith and gave him a wholehearted endorsement, calling him the "'happy Warrior' of the political battlefield."[12]

When Roosevelt completed his speech the cheering

seemed as though it would never end. It went on for an hour and thirteen minutes! Political observers agreed that Roosevelt's speech was the best of the convention.[13]

Smith did not win the Democratic nomination. The convention was deadlocked between Smith and William C. McAdoo, former secretary of the Treasury and son-in-law of former President Woodrow Wilson. After 103 ballots were counted in the steaming auditorium there was a consensus among the delegates. The nomination went to a compromise candidate from West Virginia named John W. Davis.

In November 1924, Davis lost the general election to popular Republican incumbent President Calvin Coolidge. (Harding had died in 1923 and Vice President Coolidge assumed the presidency.) But the story of the 1924 convention was Franklin Delano Roosevelt. He was back!

What made Roosevelt a political success? While at first the polio seemed to have fatally hurt his career, some speculate in hindsight that it may have actually helped it. They say that people felt sympathetic toward his condition while at the same time they admired him greatly for his strength in dealing with it. The polio helped Roosevelt cultivate an image of a fighter and leader who would not give up.[14]

Eleanor felt that the illness made him more understanding toward the hardships of others— something not easy for a person of a well-to-do background who never had a want or need for anything material. She said:

> He certainly learned to understand what suffering meant in a way that he'd never known before. And I think that grew out of his polio experience. And he certainly gained enormously in patience. That gave him some of the patience that was needed to meet the problems both of the New Deal and the war.[15]

Following his appearance at the 1924 convention, Roosevelt continued in private business. He waited patiently for his next major move, which would come in 1928.

The Honorable
Franklin D. Roosevelt

Unlike the drawn out 1924 Democratic Convention, the 1928 convention went smoothly. Again Roosevelt placed the name of New York Governor Al Smith in nomination. This time it was Roosevelt's son Elliott, then eighteen, who helped his father to the podium. And this time Al Smith received the nomination on the first ballot.

With Smith leaving his position as governor to run for President, there was a vacancy for the office. Roosevelt's friend and advisor Louis Howe thought 1928 was not the right year for Roosevelt to reenter politics. The United States had been led by Republicans for eight years and was in the midst of a prosperity boom. Howe did not anticipate it ending soon. In fact, Howe thought the powerful economy would last four more years and the Democratic nominee for President in 1932 would face certain defeat.[1]

But Democratic leaders throughout New York urged Roosevelt to run so that he could provide some balance with Smith. Smith was from New York City, while Roosevelt was from the rural Hudson Valley and was well respected in upstate New York.

There was another reason why Roosevelt was wanted. Smith was a Roman Catholic. There had never been a Catholic President (since then there has only been one, John F. Kennedy), and the 1920s were a decade of fierce anti-Catholicism. Some felt that a Catholic President would be more loyal to his church than to his country. With the Catholic Church's seat of power in the Vatican in Rome, many feared foreign influences. Others saw some corrupt labor and urban political leaders who were Catholic, and blamed all Catholics for the actions of a few.

Fellow Democrats felt that Roosevelt, a Protestant, might bring voters to the polls who might not vote for a Catholic—even in Smith's own state. Upstate New York was heavily Protestant.

Smith faced fervent bigotry nationwide, especially in the form of, but not limited to, the Ku Klux Klan (KKK). The Klan was very strong in the 1920s and claimed over 3 million members throughout the United States.[2]

Today the Klan directs its hatred toward

Franklin Roosevelt (left) was a big supporter of New York Governor
Al Smith (right), and helped Smith win the presidential nomination
in 1928.

non-Christians and non-whites. In the 1920s they were part of a nationwide distrust of Catholicism. During the 1928 campaign many Americans, along with the KKK, vented their bigotry toward Al Smith. Copies of a lie-filled book were distributed. It was called *The Awful Disclosures of Maria Monk*, which told of sexual orgies and murder in a Catholic convent. Also distributed was a fake Catholic oath ordering "war on Protestants and Masons."[3]

In Birmingham, Alabama, Ku Klux Klan members cheerfully stabbed and shot a dummy resembling Al Smith. Then they grabbed a rope and hung it from a tree to represent a lynching.[4] Not all incidents were in the South. In upstate New York a leaflet was distributed that said:

> When the Catholics rule the United States
> And the Jew grows a Christian nose on his face,
> When Pope Pius is head of the Ku-Klux-Klan
> In the land of Uncle Sam
> Then Al Smith will be our president
> And the country not worth a damn.[5]

Smith was clobbered in the 1928 election, losing to Republican Herbert Hoover, an engineer and former secretary of Commerce under Harding and Coolidge. Prejudice against Catholics certainly played a role in the election. However, with the economy booming, it is unlikely that any Democrat could have beaten Hoover in 1928. Hoover even carried Smith's New York.

Though initially cold to Roosevelt's run for the New York governorship in 1928, Louis Howe was right alongside him as the campaign's primary organizer. Roosevelt, forty-six years old, was a dynamic campaigner. He traveled by car and train throughout the state, stumping in both upstate villages and in New York City. Roosevelt was a forceful speaker with a natural ability to take facts and statistics, and turn them into lively speeches.

For example, one time he attacked the Republican's plans to transfer hydroelectric resources in New York from state control to that of private developers. Roosevelt changed what he felt was a boring lead sentence of his speech to a more commanding one: "This is a history and a sermon on the subject of water power, and I preach from the Old Testament. The text is 'Thou shalt not steal.'"[6]

All the while he was following in cousin Theodore's footsteps. Theodore Roosevelt served as governor of New York before becoming President. The governorship of a major state such as New York would give any candidate needed publicity to prepare for a Presidential race.

Amazingly, Roosevelt bucked the 1928 Republican tidal wave and was elected governor of New York, though by a slim margin. This was a testament to Roosevelt's popularity with the people of his state.

Once in office Roosevelt immediately took control and cemented his image as a powerful governor. Within the first six months he championed tax relief for farmers and cheap electric power for consumers. Roosevelt was successful.

Other progressive reforms were soon called for. Roosevelt stressed the need for statewide social programs to aid the poor, elderly, and unemployed. He was instrumental in cleaning up corrupt workmen's compensation boards, enabling laborers to choose their own doctor.

To reach as many citizens as possible, he used the power of his day's most advanced medium—radio. When opponents refused to approve Roosevelt's proposals, he addressed the public with radio talks. Often, shortly after his radio speeches, letters in support of Roosevelt appeared in large volumes in his opponents' mail.

With Roosevelt's polio limiting his mobility, Eleanor traveled with him on official state inspections. She would inspect prisons, hospitals, and asylums and report to him.

Roosevelt was a popular governor and was re-elected by a substantial margin in 1930. But the state of the country in 1930 was much different than it had been in 1928.

The United States in 1930 was in the midst of the Great Depression. In late summer and early fall of 1929 the economy showed signs of weakening. Then on

October 29, 1929, a date that would become known as Black Tuesday, the stock market "crashed."

It was on the 29th that a massive rush of stockholders, fearing that their stocks had reached peak value, sold them in a panic. The result was that the values of huge amounts of stocks suddenly became worthless. Many people lost every penny they had. One example was Jack Dempsey, a professional boxer and America's first millionaire athlete. He lost $3 million on that single day.[7]

Businesses were forced to lay off workers or to close altogether. Millions of people were suddenly unemployed, with no place to live. They literally did not know where their next meal was coming from. There was no unemployment insurance. So when people lost their jobs, their purchasing power was gone too. In turn, stores and other businesses where people had spent their money suffered or completely closed.

Others who were working barely scraped by. Once-thriving professionals had to take menial jobs to be able to eat. Workers unable to pay their rent had to give up their homes and move in with relatives.

There was no one factor that caused the Great Depression, and economists themselves disagree on specific reasons. In general it was a combination of greed, lack of foresight, and lack of regulation. In the 1920s many Americans seemed to believe that prosperity was endless and they neglected to save for future needs.

Moreover, many had the attitude that extreme wealth was a right, not a privilege.

According to author Ted Morgan, "America was the spoiled child of history, with the greatest privileged class the world had ever seen."[8] An article in the magazine *Ladies' Home Journal* summed up the attitude of the 1920s. It was titled "Everybody Ought to Be Rich."[9]

Playing the stock market was a national craze for everyone from professional brokers to storekeepers. It was legal at the time to buy stocks on credit. So many people did not have the money to back up their investments.

Another reason for the Depression was that supply had passed demand for consumer goods. Many household items we take for granted today became readily available to all people for the first time in the early 1920s. Items such as radios, toasters, washing machines, and especially automobiles, were great novelties and were greeted with excitement by consumers.

President Hoover celebrated technology, but failed to anticipate the glut of appliances and cars that flooded the market by the end of the 1920s. There was a rise in average workers' purchasing power over the course of the decade, but by the end of the 1920s the novelty of many new products had worn off. Workers were not as interested in buying them as they had been when the products first became easily available.

There was also a surplus of banks and many invested their depositors' funds unwisely. It was believed at the time that government should completely stay out of the operations of business. So there was no way to regulate how the banks spent people's money.

Roosevelt took action to deal with the hard times more quickly than any other state governor.[10] The greatest measure was the founding of the Temporary Emergency Relief Administration, known as TERA. Roosevelt realized that existing private charities and local government programs were unable to meet the needs of all those who were suddenly unemployed. Through TERA, a state-funded program, families without money were given relief in the form of about $23 a month.[11] (In today's money, $23 would equal approximately $249.) Though small, the payments were enough to keep people from starving.

This was no free handout though. The main priority of TERA was to find work for those without jobs. Only if no employment could be found would individuals then be provided food, shelter, and clothing.

By the time Roosevelt's second term as governor was ending in 1932, the economic situation in the country had become dismal. President Hoover was the target of Americans' anger.

Unemployed homeless people banded together to construct makeshift shelters of tin and cardboard. Groups of such homes were referred to as

"Hoovervilles." Empty pockets turned inside out were called "Hoover flags." Homeless people who slept outdoors covered themselves with newspapers they called "Hoover blankets."

A famous film clip from the period shows a parade of homeless men walking past a billboard reading: "Jobless Men Keep Going. We can't take care of our own."

Franklin Delano Roosevelt announced in January 1932 that he was running for President. At the Democratic National Convention in June, he was chosen as his party's nominee. Roosevelt broke with tradition by flying to Chicago to accept the nomination. Until then, party nominees stayed home to be formally notified of their selection.

While Roosevelt was planning his campaign strategy that summer, about twenty-five thousand unemployed World War I veterans gathered in Washington, D.C. These veterans were due military bonuses in 1945. Because of their desperate situations they sought their bonuses early. Since they had no place to stay in Washington, they camped in crude huts.

The Senate voted on the early bonus and rejected it. Most veterans went home, but thousands stayed in Washington. On July 28, forty veterans tried to occupy an empty building in the city of Washington. The Washington police attempted to evict the men and a brawl broke out. Shots were fired, and two veterans were killed.

Federal troops were called. Hoover placed Major General Douglas MacArthur in charge of escorting the troops out of Washington. The President instructed MacArthur to do so nonviolently. But MacArthur's men set the huts on fire, drew weapons, fired tear gas, and chased the veterans out of town. These veterans were the same men who had bravely served their country in World War I. It was an embarrassment for President Hoover in the summer of an election year.

Roosevelt campaigned hard for the presidency, but it did not matter. It was all but certain that Herbert Hoover had already lost the election.

The First
One Hundred Days

David Ginsburg, an attorney who served in two different posts during Franklin Roosevelt's administration, summed up the Great Depression. He said:

> There's only one word that adequately describes it and that's surely 'despair'. The sense of helplessness, the sense of hopelessness. . . . there was a sense of fright, a sense of horror.[1]

Roosevelt was aware of the people's "sense of fright." In his inaugural address on March 4, 1933, he confidently spoke to the American public and said these famous words:

> First of all, let me assert my firm belief that the only thing we have to fear is fear itself, nameless, unreasoning, unjustified terror, which paralyzes needed efforts to convert retreat into advance.[2]

On March 4, 1933, Franklin Delano Roosevelt was inaugurated as President of the United States.

The man who made that reassuring statement nearly did not live to see inauguration day. On February 15, when Roosevelt was President-elect and Herbert Hoover was still President, Roosevelt was in Miami to give a speech. At the completion of Roosevelt's talk the assembled crowd began to break up. Suddenly a man barely five feet tall climbed onto a bench and shot five bullets toward the President-elect.

Miraculously, Roosevelt was not hit. But five other persons were. One victim was the mayor of Chicago, Anton Cermak, who died of his injuries. The other four survived.

The case was eerily similar to the attack on President McKinley thirty-two years earlier. The would-be assassin was an immigrant American laborer named Giuseppe Zangara. Like Leon Czolgosz, McKinley's assassin, Zangara had a hatred for all government leaders. He blamed wealthy men and those he called "capitalists" for his poor health. He said that his condition was a result of having to work hard since his childhood.[3]

Theodore Roosevelt's warning to Franklin now seemed prophetic when he said, "The only real danger from an assassin is from one who does not care whether he loses his own life in the act or not."[4]

Zangara was convicted of first-degree murder and sentenced to death. As he was escorted to the electric chair, he said in broken English, "I no scared of electric chair." He commanded the prison guards, "Go ahead.

Push the button."[5] Zangara was obviously not afraid of losing his life.

There is no telling what the death of Franklin Roosevelt would have done to the spirit of the country at that moment. Almost since the instant he was elected the mood of the country changed. Although some Americans feared any changes Roosevelt might make, he was generally viewed as a vibrant enthusiastic man who believed anything was possible. The image of Herbert Hoover was that of a gloomy cheerless man overwhelmed by his job.

Most Americans could not wait until FDR took the oath of office. Some even suggested that Hoover resign immediately and let Roosevelt take over without waiting the required four months until inauguration day.[6]

In the interim between his election and his inauguration, FDR promised major changes but gave no specific details about his plans. Roosevelt spoke of a "New Deal" involving government action for the American people. He was not trying to do away with capitalism. He was trying to preserve America's capitalistic system, and he thought government regulation was necessary to do so.

Americans were not as cynical about government in the 1930s as they are today. In 1932 there was very little government activism, and most Americans thought government could be their friend. They saw FDR as their friend too.

Today the federal government insures money deposited in bank accounts. But there was no such government insurance program in 1933, and it was common for banks to fail during the Depression. This usually happened when nervous depositors, feeling their money was unsafe in a bank, withdrew it in large amounts. When banks failed, those who still had money deposited in them lost everything. Between the day of the 1932 election and the day Roosevelt took office in 1933, the closing of banks was becoming dangerously widespread. Something had to be done.

Roosevelt acted almost immediately. Two days after his inauguration he issued a proclamation declaring a four-day national bank holiday. During these four days all the nation's banks were to be closed. The bank holiday was overwhelmingly approved by both the Senate and the House of Representatives.

The primary purpose of the bank holiday was to put a stop to the avalanche of panic withdrawals and the hoarding of money. The decision was well received. In New York City, the financial center of the nation, leading bankers gave the decision their stamp of approval and said they expected success.[7]

They were right. The bank holiday served as a "cooling-off period" and eased the fears of the American public. When the banks reopened, deposits exceeded withdrawals. People began to return to the banks the money that they had been hoarding at home.

As he had done so successfully as governor of New York, Roosevelt spoke to citizens of the United States on radio. On March 12 he explained on radio the events of the previous week. This was the first of what would become known as FDR's "fireside chats."

Roosevelt opened his first such chat with the words "my friends," as he had first done on the campaign trail some thirty years earlier while running for state senate. He assured the public, adding, "I hope you can see, my friends, from this essential recital of what your government is doing that there is nothing complex, nothing radical, in the process."[8]

Soon Roosevelt's fireside chats became major events. Films taken at the time show families—parents, children, even household pets—gathered around the radio as the President spoke.

Robert Weaver, an economist from the Department of the Interior during the Roosevelt years, said of FDR, "He made listeners feel as though he was talking to them and to them individually."[9]

Weaver spoke of the President's popularity:

> I remember in those days if you went through any area during a fireside chat you could hear them [while] walking down the street. You didn't have to worry about getting home in order to hear it because it would be turned on [people's radios] all the way home.[10]

The national bank holiday was the first of many

strong actions taken by President Roosevelt in order to give the nation's economy a boost. His goal was to stabilize the system of capitalism by enacting safeguards. His method was like controlling a wild river prone to flooding with the use of dams.

Roosevelt believed that government and business could work together to avoid crises such as the Great Depression. As when he was governor of New York, FDR felt that the government should help people by creating jobs and not handing out welfare checks. However, things were so bad in the spring of 1933 that he felt federal relief was necessary to keep people from going hungry. Similar to the TERA that Governor Roosevelt established for New York, President Roosevelt created FERA (Federal Emergency Relief Administration of 1933) for the country.

But his top priority was creating jobs. In his first one hundred days of office Roosevelt and Congress created ten new government agencies that, in turn, created hundreds of thousands of new jobs. The agencies were known by some as "alphabet soup," since they were called by their acronyms. This group of federal agencies was Roosevelt's New Deal in action.

The first agency was the CCC, the Civilian Conservation Corp. It was established on March 31, less than three weeks after Roosevelt took office. The CCC put thousands to work in the nation's forests. These people planted trees, built lookout towers, and worked on flood control projects. The first CCC camp was opened in Luray, Virginia. About twenty-five thousand formerly unemployed young men between the ages of eighteen and twenty-five were at work there within one week of the camp's establishment.

More agencies formed within the first one hundred days. The list included: the AAA (Agricultural Adjustment Act), under which farmers were paid for restricting crop growth in order to reduce surpluses); the FCA (Farm Credit Administration), which provided loans to farmers facing loss of their land; and the TVA (Tennessee Valley Authority), a regional public power project on the Tennessee River.

There was also the Glass-Steagall Act, which was passed on June 16. Among other conditions, it insured savings deposits up to a specified amount. People would never again lose all their hard-earned money if a bank should fail. The Glass-Steagall Act has been credited by economists and historians for staving off a repeat of the Great Depression in the years since FDR's Administration.

Not everyone favored these early actions of the Roosevelt Administration. Critics thought that they would put the United States on the road to socialism, or at least, be harmful to capitalism. They said that businesses could excel only by competing naturally and without government interference. In their view, the

Depression would end on its own as other economic downturns had in the past.

But in 1933 these people were in the minority. The Roosevelt Administration had its own theme song for the New Deal. It was called "Happy Days Are Here Again," and it was played at Democratic conventions and political rallies. The country truly felt that if happy days were not here, they would be soon.

Mr. President

Some Presidents hated their job. But Franklin Roosevelt loved his. "He thought it was the grandest job in the world," said Roosevelt historian William Leuchtenberg.[1]

FDR's enthusiasm was infectious. In 1933 when he and Congress established a federal program called the National Recovery Administration (NRA), it was greeted with great eagerness by the public. Roosevelt considered the NRA the most important legislation passed during the early years of the New Deal.[2]

The general purpose of the NRA was to regulate business practices to make them fair to consumers, workers, and management alike. Specifically the goal was to quicken economic recovery by setting profit levels for business and wage levels for labor. There were numerous measures in the NRA. Some of the most significant were the following:

1. The NRA raised workers' wages in order to increase the amount of people able to buy goods.

2. The NRA stopped cutthroat competition and overproduction. The hope was to avoid ever again reaching the level of overproduced goods that existed in the 1920s.

3. The NRA gave each industry the right to set its own wages and prices.

4. The NRA supported the rights of workers to form unions and bargain collectively (as a group represented by a spokesman).

5. The NRA abolished child labor.

The symbol used by the government to promote the NRA was a drawing of a blue eagle above the printed words "We do our part." Before long, posters of the symbol appeared in front windows of restaurants, grocery stores, and businesses of all sorts throughout the country. The government sponsored parades in numerous cities supporting the NRA. In one parade in New York City in September 1933, over two hundred and fifty thousand people marched down busy Fifth Avenue.

The result of all the New Deal legislation was that over the next few years the economy did improve. But the country was still far from prosperous. The

Roosevelt established the National Recovery Administration (NRA) to regulate business practices and quicken an economic recovery. Its symbol was a blue eagle.

Depression was simply too deep. While new jobs were being created others were disappearing. Large numbers of American citizens were continuing to rely on welfare.

Roosevelt felt that welfare was not the answer. In 1935 he called welfare "a narcotic, a subtle destroyer of the human spirit." He also said, "The federal government must and shall quit this business of relief."[3]

As for First Lady Eleanor Roosevelt, she wanted to continue in her productive ways. She was not happy to fill only the position of official hostess as most first ladies in the past had done. She took an activist role in addition to carrying on the traditional duties of the position. She called for better conditions for oppressed workers. Eleanor traveled extensively, again acting as her husband's eyes and hands. She toured poor coal mining areas in West Virginia and examined the status of farm workers. On other trips she inspected institutions for the mentally ill.

World War I veterans camped in Washington in 1933, as they did the previous year when Herbert Hoover was President. Franklin sent Eleanor to speak with and listen to them. Impressed by her efforts, one veteran said, "Hoover sent the Army. Roosevelt sent his wife."[4]

In 1935 Congress passed Roosevelt's next major legislation, the Emergency Relief Appropriations Act. It gave the President $4.8 billion for work programs and was the largest peacetime appropriation in the history of the United States.[5]

A substantial portion of that money went to a new program in the "alphabet soup" of the New Deal called the WPA (Works Progress Administration). It would be the largest of any New Deal program.

The WPA put Americans to work. Millions of people who had been receiving welfare checks began earning paychecks. Just as importantly, these people worked in jobs and fields in which they had specific skills and training.

Under the WPA, laborers across the country built thousands of schools, hospitals, airports, roads, playgrounds, and parks. Among the projects was the famous La Guardia Airport in New York City. In total, WPA workers built hundreds of thousands of miles of roads, and thousands of schools, hospitals, playgrounds and parks.

Persons with strengths in service industries served hot lunches to schoolchildren and worked in medical clinics. Those with teaching abilities helped illiterate individuals learn to read and conducted art classes for the mentally disabled. Others with special talents took on the tedious task of transcribing millions of written pages into Braille, a special written language for the blind.

It was to Roosevelt's credit that the WPA included jobs for thousands of unemployed artists, writers, and actors. A painter and former classmate of Roosevelt

Roosevelt's Works Progress Administration (WPA) put millions of people to work. Shown here are WPA workers improving streets in Indianapolis, Indiana in 1934.

named George Biddle told the President that young artists were "eager to express . . . in living monuments the social ideals that you are struggling to achieve."[6]

The WPA's Federal Arts Projects was responsible for murals and other paintings that can still be seen today in schools, post offices, hospitals, libraries, and other public buildings. Because of their gratitude, a substantial number of WPA artists chose labor as themes of their paintings. In public buildings across the nation one might find images of riveters hard at work or men operating printing presses.

Some of those who painted while employed by the WPA became respected American artists. The list includes Ben Shahn, Jackson Pollock, and Willem de Kooning.

Among the future great writers who worked for the WPA were Ralph Ellison, Studs Terkel, Richard Wright, John Cheever, and Saul Bellow. One of the biggest projects for writers was a series of state travel guidebooks. The automobile had by then become a fixture of American life, making it easier for Americans to travel at will.

There was also the Federal Theater Project, which brought live plays to areas that had never before seen professional performances. Works were presented in Yiddish and Spanish as well as English.

At that time of expanding government, the United States was still the only industrialized country in the world without any national old-age and unemployment insurance. Wealthy elderly people had few problems making ends meet, but others had to rely on family members, charities, or poorhouses (buildings maintained for those in poverty who cannot support themselves) to get by.

Roosevelt and New Deal supporters believed that the government had a role in protecting its citizens from such dependency. In August 1935, Congress passed the Social Security Act. It provided for the same type of old-age insurance that other countries had. It also gave the same benefits to children and spouses of workers who died before reaching age sixty-five. In addition the act stated that money be returned to states so that they could establish their own systems of distributing unemployment insurance.

One item Roosevelt wanted as part of the social security package was compulsory health insurance. That, too, is found in many European countries and Canada. But Roosevelt feared the political power of groups such as the American Medical Association (AMA). He thought its opposition to such insurance would hinder the chances of the entire bill passing. So it was dropped.[7]

All this time FDR's paralysis was kept as quiet as possible. Roosevelt wore especially long pants in public to cover his leg braces. He had perfected a way of walking by holding a cane in one hand and the arm of another person in his other. Press photographers had an understanding that they would never take pictures of the President in a wheelchair. There are about twenty-five thousand photographs of Roosevelt on file at the Franklin D. Roosevelt Presidential Library in Hyde Park. Only two show him sitting in a wheelchair.[8] Political cartoonists, even those from newspapers opposing FDR's policies, never showed him as physically challenged.

A journalist named Alistair Cooke recalled:

> I don't believe five Americans in one hundred knew he was paralyzed. I think if it had been absolutely common knowledge it would have been very difficult to elect him.[9]

For relaxation and physical therapy Roosevelt continued to visit Warm Springs, Georgia. In 1932 he had his own personal cottage built on the resort grounds. Unlike the house at Campobello, a sprawling home of thirty-four rooms, the Warm Springs cottage is cozy and small with only six rooms. It looks more like a building one might find at a summer camp than a President's retreat.

It was a visit to Warm Springs that inspired Roosevelt to start another New Deal program. He noticed that people there were paying rates for electricity four times the rate he paid at Hyde Park.[10] In addition, he saw that only 10 percent of rural homes had any electricity at all. Upon returning to Washington, FDR set up the Rural Electrification Administration (REA). The REA brought electricity to farmers across America.

With electricity, farm labor became simpler and faster. As a result, farm life was revolutionized.

As any government program has, the New Deal continued to have its share of critics. Conservative businesspeople felt that government was growing too big and intruding too much into private business. People from FDR's social background called him a traitor to his class because he increased taxes on the wealthy.

On the other hand, some thought that his New Deal programs were not going far enough. One of the most prominent was a fiery priest and radio commentator from Detroit named Reverend Charles Coughlin. In addition to his fierce attacks on Roosevelt, Coughlin was a bigot who blamed the Jews for many of America's economic problems.

Another opponent was Huey P. Long, Democratic senator from Louisiana and an extremely powerful politician in the state. Long gained power by exploiting the concerns of the people he represented. He was considered a serious threat to FDR's reelection hopes in 1936—until he was assassinated in September 1935.

But not all who disagreed with Roosevelt's policies were powerful. Some were struggling businesspeople who felt that the NRA was too restricting. They believed that the NRA made it difficult for them to run their establishments and still make a comfortable profit.

In 1935 four brothers in Brooklyn, New York, who ran a poultry business were found guilty of violating

NRA regulations. The brothers then challenged the NRA as being unconstitutional and took the case to the United States Supreme Court. The nine Supreme Court Justices ruled unanimously with the poultry business. The Court said that the NRA gave the President too much power in regulating private businesses that were barely connected with interstate commerce. (The federal government does have the right to regulate true interstate commerce.) The decision made the NRA null and void.

FDR was publicly furious.[11] However, some historians feel that he was privately relieved, or at least, had mixed feelings, since the NRA had become nearly impossible to enforce.[12]

The Court decision was just the first in a long line of cases that struck down New Deal acts. But that did not deter Roosevelt from continuing with more New Deal legislation. In fact, the Social Security Act was approved by Congress a few months after the Supreme Court decision that outlawed the NRA.

By the election year 1936, unemployment was still high. Still the New Deal had created 6 million jobs and corporate profits were on the rise.[13] The economy had improved significantly in the four years since Roosevelt took office. His renomination for the presidency was a shoo-in.

Roosevelt's Republican opponent was Alf Landon, governor of Kansas. The election was a referendum on both the New Deal and Roosevelt as a person. However,

Roosevelt's friend and advisor Louis Howe was not around this time to lend a hand. He died on April 18, 1936. Howe was given a state funeral in the White House and was sorely missed by the President.[14]

But Roosevelt went ahead full-steam with his presidential campaign. Later that summer he announced, "This generation of Americans has a rendezvous with destiny."[15] The people agreed. They reelected FDR with the largest plurality ever. He received nearly 61 percent of the popular vote and 523 electoral votes. Landon won just two states, Vermont and Maine, with a total of eight electoral votes.

Jokes about the vote of Maine and Vermont abounded after the election. The theme of most jokes was that real Americans voted for Roosevelt. One political cartoon showed outlines of all the other states marching into the United States Capitol building, with outlines of Maine and Vermont crawling into a dog house. Someone wrote in capital letters on a bridge leading from New Hampshire into Maine, "YOU ARE NOW LEAVING THE UNITED STATES."[16]

The 1936 election also marked a turning point. Until that year most African Americans voted Republican. The Republican party, after all, had been the party of Abraham Lincoln. But Eleanor Roosevelt's sympathy to the plight of African Americans, along with the jobs many received from New Deal programs, changed the voting pattern. In 1936 African Americans shifted in great numbers to the Democratic party. The vast majority have been voting Democratic ever since.

One poem circulated by anti-Roosevelt bigots in 1936 was a phony dialogue between Franklin and Eleanor. It went:

> You kiss the negroes
> I'll kiss the Jews
> We'll stay in the White House
> As long as we choose . . . [17]

With the staggering support Roosevelt received in the 1936 election, he entered his second term with a burst of confidence. Perhaps he was overconfident.

The conservative United States Supreme Court was still ruling against Roosevelt's New Deal programs. Six of the nine Supreme Court Justices were over seventy years old. Four were hard-line conservatives who opposed the very concept of the New Deal.

Roosevelt pitted himself in a battle against the Supreme Court. In February 1937, he proposed that the President be permitted to add an additional Justice whenever a sitting Justice turned seventy and refused to retire within six months. (Supreme Court Justices are appointed for life.) The President would be allowed to add a maximum of six Justices.

FDR's purpose was to bring fresh thinkers to the Court. But to many, even Democrats, he was going too far. Although past Presidents had altered the total number of Justices, the number had been at nine for nearly sixty years. Roosevelt's idea seemed to many to be an attempt to "pack" the Supreme Court, or tilt the American system of checks and balances in his favor. He was said to be power hungry. The proposal became known as the "court-packing scheme."

Roosevelt fought hard for the proposal, but it was no use. The opposition was great. In July the Senate defeated the Supreme Court bill by a large margin. The defeat was a bitter one and proved to Roosevelt that he was not invincible. He could be beaten.

However, Roosevelt's proposal did seem to shake up the Court. Shortly after FDR introduced the bill, the Supreme Court switched course and approved two New Deal acts: the Social Security Act and a pro-union act called the National Labor Relations Act (also known as the Wagner Act). The Wagner Act prohibited unfair labor practices against unions and made discrimination against union members illegal.

Then one very conservative Justice, Willis Van Devanter, resigned just three months after Roosevelt first announced his plan. Over the next few years seven more Justices resigned and were replaced by more liberal New Deal supporters. In that regard Roosevelt declared victory even though Congress had voted down his proposal.[18]

Not all was rosy for Roosevelt on the economic front. The economy hit a slowdown in 1937. FDR opponents called it the Roosevelt Recession, although the situation was nowhere as desperate as it had been in 1932.

And in spite of the downturn, the basic premise of the New Deal seemed to be working. Gore Vidal, a writer and grandson of a former United States senator, said about Roosevelt, "He saved capitalism. . . . It very well could have gone under. Those who said he's a traitor to his class didn't realize he was their savior."[19]

The scariest news in the late 1930s was coming not from home, but abroad. Strong dictatorships were in power in Germany, Italy, and Japan. Worse, they were taking control of neighboring countries. By 1938 Italy had conquered Ethiopia in north Africa; Germany annexed Austria; and Japan had invaded and occupied Manchuria, a region of northeast China.

Adolf Hitler, dictator of Germany, was preaching a theory of a master race. He claimed that his race, the Aryan race, was biologically superior to all others. He viciously persecuted Jews and others whom he deemed inferior or who disagreed with him. Thousands of Jews and others had been sent to concentration camps. In Asia the Japanese were committing acts of torture against Chinese civilians.

The majority of Americans were reluctant to become involved in another war. World War I had ended less than twenty years earlier. People were concerned about their sons and brothers dying again in battles. From 1935 to 1938, Congress passed four Neutrality Acts.

These acts banned arm sales or loans from the United States to any country involved in war. This was regardless of whose side the country was on.

Roosevelt was concerned about the fascist aggression, especially in Europe. But he recognized the fact that most American citizens were strong in their opposition to war. Then in 1939 Germany invaded Poland. Soon afterward France and England, allies of Poland, declared war on Germany. World War II had begun.

In the wake of Germany's aggression, America softened its anti-war position a bit. Congress passed another Neutrality Act in November 1939. At FDR's urging, this act contained a special provision. It permitted the United States to sell supplies to France and England on a "cash and carry" basis. This meant that countries buying arms had to pay cash and carry the weapons back home on their ships.

In the spring of the next year Germany invaded Scandinavia. By the end of 1940, Germany had invaded and occupied Denmark, Norway, Holland, Luxembourg, Belgium, and France. Hitler was pursuing his terrible racist policies in these countries as well.

That year, 1940, was an election year. No President had ever run for a third term after serving two complete terms. (Theodore Roosevelt ran for a third term, but his first term was not full. He ascended to the presidency after McKinley's death and served less than four years in his first term.)

Franklin and Eleanor Roosevelt celebrated Thanksgiving in November 1939 at Warm Springs. That same month, Congress would pass another Neutrality Act containing a special provision.

In light of the turmoil in Europe, Roosevelt's supporters hoped that he would break this trend. The President himself was undecided about a third term until June, when the Nazis overran France. It was then that he decided to try for a third term.[20]

At first it appeared that the Republicans would nominate for President either Governor Thomas Dewey of New York or conservative Senator Robert Taft of Ohio. Taft was the son of former President William Howard Taft.

It was a bit of a surprise when they nominated Wendell L. Willkie. The Republican Willkie was a business executive and former Democrat with no political experience. Willkie tried running on two issues. One was that a third term would make President Roosevelt a virtual dictator of the United States. The other was that the New Deal was a failure.

Neither issue caught on with the public. Then Willkie campaigned as an anti-war candidate. He claimed that Roosevelt would lead the United States into a war. In early October he warned that a Roosevelt win would mean "wooden crosses for sons and brothers and sweethearts."[21] At one rally he asked his audience "Is there anybody here who really thinks that the President is sincerely trying to keep us out of war?"[22]

Roosevelt promised that he would keep the United States out of war unless the country was deliberately attacked. In 1940 he was reelected in another landslide.

Willkie carried only ten states to Roosevelt's 38, and received only 82 electoral votes to Roosevelt's 449. FDR received 55 percent of the popular vote to Willkie's 45 percent.

Upon being elected Roosevelt said, "We are facing difficult days in this country, but I think you will find me in the future just the same Franklin Roosevelt you have known a great many years."[23]

Mr. Commander in Chief

When Franklin Roosevelt took the oath of office for the third time on January 20, 1941, it seemed that the entire eastern hemisphere was under a cloud of war. Those lands not under foreign occupation or fighting aggressor countries were very fearful that they would be drawn into the conflict.

With the United States separated from Europe and Asia by large oceans, most Americans felt safe from the horrible fighting taking place elsewhere. Early in 1941, they still wanted nothing to do with the war "over there."

England, being an island nation, was safe from a land invasion by Germany. But in late 1940 and early 1941, the island country was mercilessly attacked from the air. Winston Churchill, the prime minister of England, had for a year been asking FDR for weapons. With these air raids continuing in full force, Churchill was getting desperate.

Roosevelt was sympathetic to England's troubles. The United States was legally able to send arms to England under the "cash and carry" arrangement. But England was bankrupt and could not pay. Roosevelt then devised an alternative plan to help England. He explained it at a press conference. He said:

> Suppose my neighbor's home catches on fire, and I have a length of garden hose four or five hundred feet away. If I can take my garden hose and connect it up with his hydrant, I may help him to put out his fire. Now what do I do? I don't say to him before that operation, "Neighbor, my garden hose cost me $15; you have to pay me $15 for it." What is the transaction that goes on? I don't want $15—I want my garden hose back after the fire is over. All right. If it goes through the fire all right, intact, without any damage to it, he gives it back to me and thanks me very much for the use of it.

If not, the President continued, it is replaced.[1]

The plan was called Lend-Lease. Roosevelt said that it was a way of keeping American men out of the war rather than getting the country closer to war. The Lend-Lease Act was approved by Congress and signed into law by the President on March 11, 1941. The United States would provide England and other Allied nations with airplanes, artillery, tanks, and guns.

Throughout 1941 the United States edged closer to war. In August, Roosevelt met with Churchill on ships off the coast of Newfoundland, a Canadian province. They composed a joint statement called the Atlantic Charter. It spelled out common objectives for both England and the United States. One was the right of self-determination for all people. Another was the right of freedom of the seas for all countries.

That fall was an eventful but tragic one for the President. His mother Sara died on September 6. Three months and one day later, on the anniversary of the death of his father, the President and the entire country were struck by startling news.

The date was Sunday, December 7, 1941. The time was about 1:30 P.M. in Washington, D.C. It was about 7:30 A.M. in faraway Pearl Harbor, Hawaii, the site of a large American naval base.

The President had planned to spend the Sunday afternoon relaxing with his stamp collection.[2] The First Lady was stepping into a White House hall to say goodbye to guests. And the men on the battleships, destroyers, and light cruisers at Pearl Harbor were sleeping, reading the Sunday newspaper, or eating breakfast.

Secretary of the Navy Frank Knox walked into the President's study where the President was sitting with one of his most trusted advisors, Harry Hopkins. Knox announced to Roosevelt, "Mr. President, it looks like the Japanese have attacked Pearl Harbor."[3]

Hopkins found it hard to believe and thought that the news was a mistake.[4] But within a half hour, the bloody attack was confirmed.

The President wired the news to Churchill in England. Churchill responded by calling the President on the telephone. Churchill said, "Mr. President, what's this about Japan?" Roosevelt replied, "It's quite true. They have attacked us at Pearl Harbor. We are all in the same boat now."[5]

The destruction was devastating. One naval seaman named Donald Stratton, stationed on the battleship USS *Arizona*, said of his ship. "That battleship weighed 35,000 tons and it just shook like a piece of paper. We were all trapped in that ball of flame."[6]

Stratton was lucky; he survived. A total of 2,403 American servicemen died in the Pearl Harbor attack. Over eleven hundred were wounded.[7]

The people of the United States who had felt so strongly about staying out of the war were now outraged. The next day Roosevelt went on the radio and asked Congress to declare war on Japan.

With words that are now famous he said, "Yesterday, December 7, 1941—a date which will live in infamy—the United States of America was suddenly and deliberately attacked by naval and air forces of the empire of Japan."[8]

Four days later Germany and Italy, in support of Japan, declared war on the United States. Americans were suddenly united in their support of their country's involvement in World War II. Roosevelt declared that "Dr. New Deal" had been replaced by "Dr. Win-the-War."

Today the Allied victory is taken for granted. But in late 1941 and early 1942, the situation looked bleak. There were no guarantees that the Allies—mainly the United States, Canada, Britain, France, and Australia— would win. Some Americans felt that Germany was too strong for the Allies to have a chance to win.

In December 1941, Germany occupied most of Europe and was invading Russia. Italy and its German allies occupied most of north Africa. By the middle of 1942 Japan would occupy most of the islands in the Pacific and much of China.

Under Roosevelt's orders American industry got busy producing the tools of war. Auto manufacturers made tanks instead of pleasure cars. Garment businesses made parachutes instead of stockings. Mandatory rationing was in effect for the purchase of meat, sugar, gasoline, rubber, and other foods and goods needed for the important war effort.

The extensive war production did something the New Deal could not completely do. It finally pulled the nation out of the Depression. With the great demands for products for the war effort, anyone who wanted a job could find one.

Churchill came from England to Washington in late 1941 and moved into the White House. He stayed about a month and discussed military options with the President. Roosevelt's idea was to launch an attack from south England across the English Channel into France. His goal was to liberate the French from the German occupation.

Churchill did not think the allies were adequately trained for that immense job. Instead, they decided to jointly invade North Africa. The action would be called Operation Torch. The purpose was to free the countries of North Africa from their Italian and German occupiers. On November 8, 1942, over ninety thousand American and British fighting men stormed the beaches of North Africa.[9]

Two months later Roosevelt traveled to North Africa to meet again with Churchill and plan further courses of action. The two met in the city of Casablanca in Morocco. Since the two men were meeting in a war zone, there were many security concerns. There was no telling what disaster could occur if the Germans found out about the presence of the two leaders.

It was later learned that the Germans did know the location of the meeting was Casablanca. However, the name *Casablanca* in Spanish means "white house." Hitler therefore thought that the meeting was being held

In January, 1943, Franklin Roosevelt (seated, left) met with British
Prime Minister Winston Churchill (seated, right) in Casablanca.

at the White House in distant Washington, D.C.—too far away for an attack.[10]

The entire journey was a brave move on Roosevelt's part. He took time to visit American troops stationed in Morocco. By doing so he became the first President since Abraham Lincoln to visit American troops in a combat zone. Upon seeing the President, one soldier said, "Gosh—it's the old man himself!"[11] The President laughed good-naturedly in response.

The decision to launch a cross-channel invasion was again postponed. Instead, Churchill and Roosevelt planned an invasion of Sicily, an Italian island. It is located at Italy's southern tip in the Mediterranean Sea.

Allied forces invaded Sicily in July 1943. Italy's dictator Benito Mussolini was overthrown by his people, and Italy surrendered to the Allies. But the fighting in Italy continued. Germans filled the vacuum left by withdrawing Italian forces.

By the autumn of 1943, the war in North Africa, for the most part, was over. The large region had been liberated.

Americans were also fighting throughout the Pacific. In 1942 the Allies lost the Philippines to Japan. But later that year the Allies won pivotal battles in the Coral Sea off Australia and near a Pacific island called Midway.

Meanwhile, anti-Japanese hysteria gripped America. These feelings extended to American citizens of Japanese ancestry. Some people feared that California might become the next Pearl Harbor. Others were simply racist. But most questioned the loyalty of all persons of Japanese ancestry.

Early in 1942, under pressure from worried Americans, Roosevelt signed an order forcing one hundred and ten thousand persons of Japanese ancestry living on the West Coast to leave. They suddenly had to sell their homes, businesses, and property or leave them in the hands of others. Eventually they were placed in ten relocation camps. Eight camps were in the wide open spaces of the West, but two were located in the muggy swamps of Arkansas.

Roosevelt did seem concerned about the internees' well-being. First Lady Eleanor Roosevelt made a personal visit to an internment camp in Arizona to inspect conditions and show the internees that they were not being ignored. She was busy on other journeys too. Wartime trips took her to England, the Caribbean, and the Pacific. Yet she never lost interest in the President's New Deal programs. She even expressed regret that the President put New Deal programs on the back burner during the war.[12]

But the war continued to be Roosevelt's top priority. In November 1943, in Tehran, Iran, Roosevelt again met with Churchill. This time they were joined by Josef Stalin, dictator of the Soviet Union. Because Stalin was fighting against Nazi Germany he, too, was on the side of the Allies.

President Franklin Roosevelt (center) met in November 1943 with Soviet Premier Josef Stalin (left) and British Prime Minister Winston Churchill (right). The meeting took place in Tehran, Iran.

Stalin had been pressing hard for England and the United States to launch the cross-channel invasion. Such an invasion would force the Germans to withdraw some soldiers from Russia and redirect them to a new second front.

The cross-channel invasion had been postponed for nearly two years. Now it was time. The invasion would take place on the beaches in a region of northern France called Normandy. It would be called Operation Overlord. Churchill and Roosevelt promised that it would take place within six months.

On June 6, 1944, known as D-Day, Operation Overlord was launched. It was the largest naval attack in the history of the world. Over fifty-four hundred ships and landing craft took part. And 156,000 men—the size of the population of a medium-sized city—had landed on the beaches by day's end.[13] The effort was truly an enormous one.

So was the toll. A total of ninety-five hundred men fighting for the Allies were killed or wounded on D-Day.[14] Many were just eighteen or nineteen years old.

But overall the invasion was successful. D-Day marked the beginning of the end of the war. Except for one German counterattack called the Battle of the Bulge in the winter of 1944–45, the Allies constantly moved forward. They liberated France, then pushed the Nazis back to Germany. In the meantime, on the eastern front, the Soviet Union also steadily moved against Germany.

In the Pacific the Allies took one island after another that had been controlled by Japan.

A presidential election was held that fall. It was the first wartime presidential election in the United States in eighty years. Roosevelt ran for a fourth term against New York Governor Thomas Dewey. Again the issue of too many terms in the White House was raised. In addition, rumors of the President's poor health spread throughout the nation.

But the President never lost his sense of humor. He still knew how to charm audiences. Republican opponents had circulated a story that FDR sent a Navy destroyer to the Aleutian Islands in Alaska for the sole purpose of rescuing his pet Scottish terrier, Fala. They said the dog was left behind after a presidential visit. In a speech in September, FDR used the episode to blast the Republican attacks on his family.

By today's standards, the speech might be perceived as offensive toward Scots. But this was the 1940s, not the 1990s, and sensitivity toward ethnic groups was not a major issue. In FDR's time his speech was not seen as offensive.

Roosevelt said, "These Republican leaders have not been content with attacks on me, or on my wife, or on my sons. No, not content with that, they now include my little dog, Fala."

The audience laughed.

The President continued, "Well, of course, I don't

resent attacks, and my family doesn't resent attacks, but Fala *does* resent them."

There were more roars of laughter.

Roosevelt went on. "You know—you know—Fala's Scotch, and being a Scottie, as soon as he learned that the Republican fiction writers, in Congress and out, had concocted a story that I had left him behind on an Aleutian island and had sent a destroyer back to find him—at a cost to the taxpayers of two or three, or eight or twenty million dollars, his Scotch soul was furious. He has not been the same dog since."[15]

The room thundered with laughter.

Again, Roosevelt won the election in a landslide. The President won 38 states to Dewey's 12, with 432 electoral votes to Dewey's 99. Roosevelt received a bit over 53 percent of the popular vote, and Dewey earned a little less than 46 percent.

The twin trials of the Depression and the war had taken their toll on FDR's health. The President was looking thin and tired. He fell asleep during conversations and complained of headaches. A medical examination in March 1944, showed that he had an enlarged heart.

The President's personal doctor, along with a group of Navy doctors, placed him on a recovery program. It included a low-fat diet, more rest, fewer cigarettes, and regular doses of a medicine called digitalis to improve his heart condition.[16]

Regardless of health concerns, Roosevelt was still President of the United States and had duties to fulfill. From February 4 through 11, 1945, Roosevelt met again with Churchill and Stalin at a seaport in the Soviet Union called Yalta.

Germany and Japan were steadily losing ground, and it was obvious the war would be over within a matter of months. The purpose of the meeting was to discuss the final plans for Germany's defeat and the political situation in the post-war world.

Several deals were made at Yalta. By the time of the meeting, the Soviet Union had liberated most of eastern Europe from Nazi control and was occupying those countries. One such country was Poland. In order to gain Stalin's help in defeating Japan, Roosevelt allowed Stalin to keep Poland as long as there were free elections. Stalin agreed. Unfortunately he did not keep his word regarding free elections in Poland, or in any of the other eastern European countries under the Soviet Union's control.

Roosevelt's deals with Stalin at Yalta are still a source of debate among historians. Some blame Roosevelt for "selling out" Poland and the rest of eastern Europe to the Soviet Union. They say that Roosevelt's poor health interfered with his ability to negotiate strongly with Stalin. They insist that a healthier President would never have let the communist Soviet Union control eastern Europe (which they did until the fall of communism in Europe in the late 1980s).

Franklin Roosevelt was buried at his home in Hyde Park, New York.

Others say that Roosevelt did the best he could under the circumstances. They argue that the Soviets were already in eastern Europe when the Yalta meeting took place, and Roosevelt could not realistically expect them to leave. Meanwhile the Allies needed Soviet help to end the war in the Pacific as soon as possible. FDR's supporters say that he made the deal with Stalin because he thought it would shorten the war.

In his speech to Congress following the Yalta conference, a weary President Roosevelt made his only public reference ever to his physical handicap. He announced:

> I hope that you will pardon me for an unusual posture of sitting down during the presentation of what I want to say. But I know that you will realize that it makes it a lot easier for me in not having to carry about ten pounds of steel round on the bottom of my legs, and also because of the fact that I have just completed a 14,000-mile trip.[17]

Franklin Delano Roosevelt did not live to see the post-war world. While having his portrait painted at his retreat in Warm Springs, he suffered a massive cerebral hemorrhage. He died hours later. The date was April 12, 1945, and he was sixty-three years old.

After a funeral service in the East Room of the White House, Franklin Delano Roosevelt was buried at his home in Hyde Park, New York.

9

Legacy and Aftermath

After President Roosevelt died, Vice President Harry Truman was sworn in as President. Truman was reelected in 1948 and served nearly eight years in office.

German dictator Adolf Hitler committed suicide on April 30, 1945. Germany surrendered to the Allies on May 8, ending the war in Europe. The war in the Pacific continued through the summer. On August 6 the United States dropped an atomic bomb, destroying the city of Hiroshima, Japan. Three days later the United States dropped a second atomic bomb, destroying the city of Nagasaki. On August 14 President Truman announced the surrender of Japan. On September 2 Japan formally surrendered. World War II was finally over.

The Japanese Americans held in internment camps

were released in 1945. In 1976 President Gerald Ford issued an official proclamation condemning the act of internment. In 1988 Congress authorized monetary compensation to those who were evacuated, relocated, or interned during the war.

Upon the liberation of the concentration camps in Europe, it was learned that Hitler and the Nazi regime had systematically murdered over 11 million people. The majority, a total of 6 million, were Jews. The other 5 million included Jehovah's Witnesses, homosexuals, communists, gypsies, and political opponents.

The League of Nations, which was such an important issue in the 1920 presidential election, foundered without American membership. It was not effective and finally was dissolved in 1946. In his last years Roosevelt pushed for the formation of a similar but stronger organization called the United Nations. At a conference in San Francisco, the UN was officially chartered on October 24, 1945.

Eleanor Roosevelt lived for seventeen years after her husband's death. She became a diplomat and was widely known as a humanitarian. She had a long association with the United Nations and chaired the UN Commission on Human Rights. In that role she spearheaded the adoption of the "Universal Declaration of Human Rights." She worked actively until her death on November 7, 1962.

Roosevelt's five surviving children are all now

deceased. The four sons all served active duty during World War II and won several military honors.

The only daughter, Anna Roosevelt Dall Boettiger, shared many of her mother's views—especially in fighting to end racial and gender discrimination. She worked as editor of the women's page of the *Seattle Post-Intelligencer* and once co-hosted a radio discussion show with her mother. She died on December 1, 1975.

James Roosevelt was his father's private secretary before serving six terms as a congressman from Los Angeles. He then operated a private consulting business in southern California. He died on August 13, 1991.

Elliott Roosevelt had a career in advertising and radio before being elected mayor of Miami Beach, Florida. He wrote fourteen books, including a series of mysteries featuring his mother as the central character. He died on October 27, 1990.

Franklin Roosevelt, Jr., was an attorney and congressman from New York. He later served as undersecretary of commerce for Presidents Kennedy and Johnson, then as chairman of the Equal Opportunity Commission for Johnson. He died on August 17, 1988, which coincidentally, was his seventy-fourth birthday.

John Roosevelt was the only son not to seek elective office. He also parted from family loyalties by becoming a Republican. A financier and generous philanthropist, he died on April 27, 1981.

Surprising to many, cousin Taddy's marriage was a

success and lasted until his wife's death in 1940. Taddy then lived alone until his death in 1958.

President Roosevelt's New Deal policies were expanded or maintained by each succeeding President through Jimmy Carter. Harry Truman extended New Deal measures with a program that he called the Fair Deal. Dwight Eisenhower, the only Republican elected between 1932 and 1968, expanded social security. Eisenhower also supported a major public works program—the building of what became the Interstate Highway System.

John F. Kennedy proposed expanding social welfare legislation in a program that he called the New Frontier. Lyndon Johnson's domestic program was called the Great Society. Under it, Congress established Medicare, which provided medical care for all persons over age sixty-five. A federal program aimed at aiding schools and libraries was also passed. Richard Nixon established the Environmental Protection Agency (EPA) and proposed a huge program to clean up water pollution in the United States.

Under Gerald Ford and Jimmy Carter there were no major expansions of New Deal-type policies. But neither tried to dismantle existing programs.

The election of President Ronald Reagan in 1980 signaled a trend away from government involvement in regulating business and providing assistance for needy persons. The trend continues. George Bush followed Reagan's basic philosophy.

Democrat Bill Clinton was elected in 1992. At the time of his election, polls showed that Americans felt that the cost of health care was too expensive for the average working person to afford. President Clinton and his wife Hillary Rodham Clinton, an activist first lady like Eleanor Roosevelt, tried to pass a system of national health insurance just as FDR had considered in the 1930s. (Harry Truman also proposed a similar program in the late 1940s.) However, a massive lobbying effort by opponents, such as major insurance and business associations, helped defeat the plan.

In the mid-term elections of 1994, the Republicans won control of both houses of Congress for the first time in forty years. They campaigned on a platform calling for even fewer government social programs and less regulation of business. In his State of the Union address in January 1995, Clinton promised to downsize government.

Some say that this trend proves that the New Deal was a bad idea, and the country is finally getting on the right track. Others say that the New Deal was a good idea and the country is on the wrong track. Still others say that the New Deal worked in its time but is outdated for the United States in the 1990s. They argue that the United States is a different country today than it was in the 1930s, and programs of that type are no longer necessary.

The majority of historians believe that Franklin Roosevelt was one of the country's truly great Presidents. They feel that he used intelligence, foresight, compassion, and courage in both saving America's capitalist system in the 1930s and helping to save the free world in the 1940s.

Fifty years later politicians continued to refer to Franklin Roosevelt when speaking of great leaders. At the 1984 Democratic Convention, Jesse Jackson drew applause when he said that he would rather have FDR in a wheelchair than Ronald Reagan on a horse. Yet Ronald Reagan, a conservative Republican, compared himself to Roosevelt in his acceptance speech at the 1980 Republican National Convention.

Reagan told his audience that he was going to speak the words of a past President, but did not give any name. He then quoted the past President, saying, " . . . 'I propose to you, my friends, and through you, that government of all kinds, big and little, be made solvent and that the example be set by the President of the United States and his cabinet.' End of quote."

Reagan continued, "That was Franklin Delano Roosevelt's words as he accepted the Democratic nomination for President in 1932."[1]

Even ultra-conservative Speaker of the House Newt Gingrich praised Roosevelt in 1995, calling FDR "the greatest President of the twentieth century, maybe of all time."[2]

In 1982 over eight hundred historians took part in a national poll ranking the American Presidents according to greatness. Franklin Roosevelt finished second, behind Abraham Lincoln. George Washington finished third.[3]

The most moving tribute to Franklin Roosevelt may have been given by Jonas Salk. Salk was the scientist who developed the vaccine that cured polio, the ailment that afflicted the President and greatly altered his life. Salk said of FDR:

> He was a man of indomitable spirit, and the combination of these two events [polio and World War II], plus the challenge that the war afforded, provided him with a kind of adversity that's like a challenge to climb Mount Everest. But he had it in him to do that.
>
> And he did it with consummate grace and great wisdom. And I'll always remember hearing his voice saying, 'There's nothing to fear but fear itself.' And that freedom from fear is a message that still rings in my ears when I think of Franklin Roosevelt and the problems of our time.[4]

Chronology

1882—Born in Hyde Park, New York, on January 30.

1896—Attends Groton School in Groton,
-1900 Massachusetts.

1900—Attends and graduates from Harvard University.
-1904

1905—Marries Anna Eleanor Roosevelt on March 17.

1906—Daughter Anna Eleanor is born.

1907—Son James is born.

1909—Son Franklin, Jr., is born; dies seven months later.

1910—Eelected to New York State Senate; son Elliott is born.

1912—Named assistant secretary of the Navy by newly elected President Woodrow Wilson.

1914—Fourth son, the second named Franklin, Jr., is born.

1916—Son John is born.

1920—Runs for Vice President on Democratic ticket; loses in general election in November.

1921—Contracts polio at Campobello.

1924—Reenters public life as he gives nominating speech for New York Governor Al Smith at Democratic National Convention; first visit to Warm Springs, Georgia.

1928—Elected governor of New York.

1930—Reelected governor of New York.

1932—Elected President of the United States.

1933—Narrowly escapes assassination; introduces sweeping New Deal legislation in first one hundred days.

1935—Introduces more major New Deal programs, including Works Progress Administration and Social Security Act.

1935—United States Supreme Court declares a New Deal program, the National Recovery Act, unconstitutional.

1936—Reelected President of the United States in a landslide.

1937—Attempt to increase number of sitting Supreme Court Justices is defeated.

1939—Neutrality Act with "cash and carry" provision is passed.

1940—Reelected President of the United States for a third term.

1941—Lend-Lease act is passed; meets British Prime Minister Winston Churchill off coast of Newfoundland and issues Atlantic Charter; United States enters World War II on December 8.

1942—Operation Torch is launched.

1943—Conference with Churchill at Casablanca.

1943—Conference with Churchill and Soviet Union Premier Josef Stalin in Tehran; Operation Overlord is planned.

1944—Operation Overlord is launched on June 6; reelected President of the United States for a fourth term.

1945—Conference with Churchill and Stalin at Yalta; dies on April 12.

Places to Visit

Hyde Park, New York

Home of Franklin D. Roosevelt National Historic Site.
This is the mansion where Franklin Roosevelt was born and lived much of his adult life. Also here are the Roosevelts' gravesites. Open year-round. (Adjacent to the property is Val-Kill, Eleanor Roosevelt's home where she lived after the President's death.) (914) 229-9115.

Franklin D. Roosevelt Library and Museum.
The official Roosevelt presidential museum includes displays ranging from the President's car to original drafts of his speeches to a high-tech exhibit about World War II. (914) 229-8114.

Campobello Island, New Brunswick, Canada

Roosevelt Campobello International Park.
The highlight of the park is the Roosevelt summer home, where FDR was stricken with polio. The island is connected to the state of Maine by the Franklin D. Roosevelt Memorial Bridge. Open late May through early October. (506) 752-2922.

Warm Springs, Georgia

Little White House State Historic Site.
The place where FDR went for polio therapy treatments is also the site of his death. You can tour Roosevelt's cottage, which looks as it did on April 12, 1945. Open year-round. (706) 655-5870.

Washington, D.C.

The White House.
Several rooms in the official residence of the sitting United States President are open to visitors. Free tours are offered Tuesday through Saturday, 10 A.M. to noon. You can get tickets on the day of your tour, or in advance through the office of your senator or congressperson. (202) 456-7041.

Chapter Notes

Chapter 1

1. Russell D. Buhite and David W. Levy, *FDR's Fireside Chats* (New York: Penguin Books, 1993), p. 5.

2. Nathan Miller, *F.D.R.: An Intimate History* (Garden City, N.Y.: Doubleday & Co., Inc., 1983), p. 289.

3. Herbert J. Cohen, *Page One* (New York: Arno Press, 1981), p. 52.

4. James Roosevelt and Sidney Shalett, *Affectionately, FDR* (New York: Harcourt, Brace & Co., 1959), p. 232.

Chapter 2

1. Nathan Miller, *F.D.R.: An Intimate History* (Garden City, N.Y.: Doubleday & Co., Inc., 1983), p. 7.

2. Geoffrey Ward, *Before the Trumpet: Young Franklin Roosevelt 1882–1905* (New York: Harper & Row Publishers, 1985), 110.

3. Miller, p. 16.

4. Ward, p. 124.

5. Miller, p. 22.

6. Ibid., p. 17.

7. Ward, p. 141.

8. Ibid., p. 177.

9. Ibid., p. 184.

10. Ted Morgan, *FDR: A Biography* (New York: Simon & Schuster, Inc., 1985), p. 62.

11. Miller, p. 28.

12. Eleanor Roosevelt, *This Is My Story* (New York: Harper and Brothers, 1937), p. 11.

13. Roosevelt, pp. 17–18.

14. Ibid., p. 18.

15. Ibid., p. 11.

16. Ibid., p. 51.

17. Joseph P. Lash, *Eleanor and Franklin* (New York: W.W. Norton & Co., Inc., 1971), p. 101.

Chapter 3

1. Geoffrey Ward, *Before the Trumpet: Young Franklin Roosevelt 1882–1905* (New York: Harper & Row Publishers, 1985), p. 217.

2. Ibid., p. 219.

3. Nathan Miller, *F.D.R.: An Intimate History* (Garden City, N.Y.: Doubleday & Co., Inc., 1983), p. 35.

4. Ibid.

5. Ted Morgan, *FDR: A Biography* (New York: Simon & Schuster, Inc., 1985), p. 79.

6. Ward, p. 252.

7. Ibid., p. 253.

8. Ibid., p. 254.

9. Ibid., p. 251.

10. Ibid., p. 340.

11. Joseph Alsop, *FDR 1882–1945: A Centenary Remembrance* (New York: The Viking Press, 1982), p. 61.

12. Ibid., p. 64.

13. Joseph P. Lash, *Eleanor and Franklin* (New York: W.W. Norton & Co., Inc., 1971), pp. 220, 226.

14. Kenneth S. Davis, *FDR: The Beckoning of Destiny, 1882–1928, A History* (New York: G.P. Putnam's Sons, 1971), p. 624.

Chapter 4

1. Personal interview with Leslie Watson, December 30, 1994.

2. Ibid.

3. *The American Experience: FDR*, television program, David Grubin Productions, Inc., PBS, 1994.

4. Joseph P. Lash, *Eleanor and Franklin* (New York: W.W. Norton & Co., Inc., 1971), p. 273.

5. *The American Experience: FDR*, television program, David Grubin Productions, Inc., PBS, 1994.

6. Nathan Miller, *F.D.R.: An Intimate History* (Garden City, N.Y.: Doubleday & Co., Inc., 1983), pp. 190–191.

7. Paul F. Boller, Jr., *Presidential Wives: An Anecdotal History* (New York: Oxford University, 1988), p. 290.

8. Joseph Alsop, *FDR: A Centenary Remembrance* (New York: The Viking Press, 1982), p. 95.

9. James Roosevelt and Sidney Shalett, *Affectionately, FDR* (New York: Harcourt, Brace & Company, 1959) p. 187.

10. Ibid., p. 205.

11. Ibid., p. 206.

12. David C. Whitney, *The American Presidents* (Garden City, N.Y.: Doubleday & Co., Inc., 1978), p. 287.

13. Miller, p. 205.

14. Arthur P. Molella and Elsa M. Burton, *FDR: The Intimate Presidency* (Washington, D.C.: National Museum of American History, Smithsonian Institution, 1982), p. 13.

15. *The American Experience: FDR*, television program, David Grubin Productions, Inc., PBS, 1994.

Chapter 5

1. Joseph Alsop, *FDR: A Centenary Remembrance* (New York: The Viking Press, 1982), p. 103.

2. Allan Nevins and Henry Steele Commager, *A Pocket History of the United States* (New York: Pocket Books, 1981), p. 411.

3. Paul F. Boller, Jr., *Presidential Campaigns* (New York: Oxford University Press, 1985), p. 228.

4. Ibid., p. 229.

5. Ibid., pp. 228–229.

6. Nathan Miller, *F.D.R.: An Intimate History* (Garden City, N.Y.: Doubleday & Co., Inc., 1983), pp. 223–224.

7. Richard Norton Smith, Maureen H. Harding, and Timothy Alch, *Herbert Hoover Library & Museum: A Guide to the Museum Galleries* (West Branch, Iowa: Herbert Hoover Library and Museum, 1993), p. 51.

8. Ted Morgan, *FDR: A Biography* (New York: Simon & Schuster, Inc., 1985), p. 317.

9. Ibid.

10. Alsop, p. 103.

11. Miller, p. 256.

Chapter 6

1. *The American Experience: FDR*, television program, David Grubin Productions, Inc., PBS, 1994.

2. Franklin D. Roosevelt Library, *Speeches of FDR*, audiotape.

3. George Sullivan, *They Shot the President* (New York: Scholastic, Inc., 1993), p. 89.

4. Ted Morgan, *FDR: A Biography* (New York: Simon & Schuster, Inc., 1985), p. 79.

5. Sullivan, p. 99.

6. Nathan Miller, *F.D.R.: An Intimate History* (Garden City, N.Y.: Doubleday & Co., Inc., 1983), p. 292.

7. Herbert J. Cohen, *Page One* (New York: Arno Press, 1981), p. 54.

8. Russell D. Buhite and David W. Levy, *FDR's Fireside Chats* (New York: Penguin Books, 1993), p. 16.

9. *The Great Depression*, television program, volume 3, Blackside, Inc. Productions, PBS, 1993.

10. Ibid.

Chapter 7

1. *The American Experience: FDR*, television program, David Grubin Productions, Inc., PBS, 1994.

2. Joseph Alsop, *FDR: A Centenary Remembrance* (New York: The Viking Press, 1982), p. 123.

3. Nathan Miller, *F.D.R.: An Intimate History* (Garden City, N.Y.: Doubleday & Co., Inc., 1983), p. 366.

4. Paul E. Boller, Jr., *Presidential Wives: An Anecdotal History* (New York: Oxford University Press, 1988), p. 293.

5. *The Great Depression*, television program, volume 3, Blackside, Inc. Productions, PBS, 1993.

6. Arthur P. Molella and Elsa M. Burton, *FDR: The Intimate Presidency* (Washington, D.C.: National Museum of American History, Smithsonian Institution, 1982), p. 30.

7. Miller, p. 374.

8. Franklin D. Roosevelt Library, Hyde Park, N.Y.

9. *The American Experience: FDR*, television program, David Grubin Productions, Inc., PBS, 1994.

10. *Franklin D. Roosevelt's Little White House and Museum* (Atlanta: Department of Natural Resources, Parks, Recreation & Historic Sites Division), p. 4.

11. Ted Morgan, *FDR: A Biography* (New York: Simon & Schuster, Inc. 1985), p. 422.

12. Ibid., pp. 422–423 and correspondence from Professor Clayton Brown, Texas Christian University, March 15, 1995.

13. *The American Experience: FDR*, television program, David Grubin Productions, Inc., PBS, 1994.

14. Kenneth S. Davis, *FDR The New Deal Years 1933–1937* (New York: Random House, 1986), pp. 602–603.

15. Franklin D. Roosevelt Library, *Speeches of FDR*, audiotape.

16. Paul F. Boller, Jr., *Presidential Campaigns* (New York: Oxford University Press, 1985), p. 249.

17. Joseph P. Lash, *Eleanor and Franklin* (New York: W.W. Norton & Co., Inc., 1971), p. 446.

18. Alsop, p. 162.

19. *The Great Depression* television program, volume 3, Blackside, Inc. Productions, PBS, 1993.

20. Alsop, p. 202.

21. Boller, *Presidential Campaigns*, p. 253.

22. Ibid.

23. Herbert H. Cohen, *Page One* (New York: Arno Press, 1981), p. 101.

Chapter 8

1. *Complete Presidential Press Conferences of Franklin D. Roosevelt* (New York: Da Capo Press, 1972), vol. 16, p. 354.

2. James Roosevelt and Sidney Shalett, *Affectionately, FDR* (New York: Harcourt, Brace & Company, 1959), p. 328.

3. Doris Kearns Goodwin, *Franklin and Eleanor Roosevelt: The Home Front in World War II, No Ordinary Time* (New York: Simon & Schuster, 1994), p. 289.

4. Ibid.

5. Ibid., p. 290.

6. "Remembering Pearl Harbor," *Newsweek*, November 25, 1991, p. 35.

7. Personal correspondence from Franklin D. Roosevelt Library, dated May 23, 1995.

8. James L. Whitehead, *The Museum of the Franklin D. Roosevelt Library*, booklet, p. 12.

9. Burns, p. 291.

10. Goodwin, pp. 401, 402.

11. Ibid., p. 405.

12. Joseph Lash, *"Life Was Meant to be Lived": A Centenary Portrait of Eleanor Roosevelt* (New York: W.W. Norton and Co., 1984), p. 114.

13. "D Day By the Numbers," *USA Today*, June 7, 1994, p. 3A.

14. Ibid.

15. Franklin D. Roosevelt Library, *Speeches of FDR*, audiotape.

16. Burns, pp. 448–449.

17. Franklin D. Roosevelt Library, *Speeches of FDR*, audiotape.

Chapter 9

1. "Text of Reagan's Speech Accepting the Republicans' Nomination," *New York Times*, July 18, 1980, p. A8.

2. Martin E. Nolan, "FDR's Legacy Resonates Still," *The Boston Globe*, April 9, 1995, p. 30.

3. Robert K. Murray and Tim H. Blessing, "The Presidential Performance Study: A Progress Report," *The Journal of American History*, December 1983, p. 540.

4. *Class of the Twentieth Century*, television program, volume 3, CEL Communications, Inc. and Arts and Entertainment Network, 1991.

Further Reading

Allen, Peter. *The Origins of World War II*. New York: The Bookwright Press, 1992.

Bredeson, Carmen. *Jonas Salk: Discoverer of the Polio Vaccine*. Hillside, N.J.: Enslow Publishers, 1993.

Lawson, Don. *FDR's New Deal*. New York: Thomas W. Crowell, 1979.

Meltzer, Milton. *Brother, Can You Spare a Dime?* New York: Alfred A. Knopf, 1969.

Roosevelt, Eleanor. *This I Remember*. New York: Harper & Brothers, 1949.

————. *This Is My Story*. New York: Harper & Brothers, 1937.

Roosevelt, James, and Sidney Shalett. *Affectionately, FDR*. New York: Harcourt, Brace & Company, 1959.

Stanley, Jerry. *Children of the Dust Bowl*. New York: Crown Publishers, Inc., 1992.

Index